Write to Publish

Essentials for the Modern Fiction & Memoir Market

Also by Christopher Klim

Jesus Lives in Trenton, Creative Arts Books, 2002
ISBN 0-88739-418-3

"Understated humor and lack of pretension lend this wry urban fable undeniable charm. ... Klim's lighthearted entertainment possesses genuine heart."
　　　—*Will Hickman,* **Booklist**, *February 2002*

"Christopher Klim is that rare talent who brings characters and stories that resonate with the working class and excite the sensibilities of literary connoisseurs. Maybe he's the New Jersey reincarnation of John Steinbeck. More likely he's destined to become someone quite unique in the pantheon of American novelists."
　　　—*Robert Gover, author of* **One Hundred Dollar Misunderstanding**

"Klim has a colorful past, and it comes to life in the pages of Jesus Lives in Trenton, which has an ear for realistic dialogue and an eye for city grit that would make Dashiell Hammett Proud ..."
　　　—*Katie Haegele,* **Philadelphia Weekly**

"It all comes together in a compelling and funny new novel called JESUS LIVES IN TRENTON."
　　　—*Mark Drucker,* **KYW News Radio Philadelphia**

"Boot Means is no ordinary man. ... Klim drew upon his personal experiences to bring Boot Means to life."
　　　—*Tammy Paolino,* **The Home News Tribune**

"The book is indeed a riotously funny, quick read. It also works on a deeper level, serving as an allegory about man's thirst for grace in a chaotic world."
—*Matt Smith,* **Time Off**

"[Klim] has managed to stake his claim amid a welter of clever plot twists, machine-gun dialog, and generally amusing scenarios. ... this book was such a damn good read, I am going to pretend to my editor that it got lost in the mail, and keep this review copy for myself. It'll look good on my shelves. ... -- nestled snugly in between Seth Morgan's Homeboy and Robert Stone's Dog Soldiers."
—*Jason Price Everett,* **The Circle Magazine**

"Laced with the first hints of satiric leanings from its opening volley, Jesus Lives in Trenton is clear about its intentions from the start: its first and foremost goal is to entertain ... Jesus Lives in Trenton is laden with laughs, insight and an overflowing abundance of literary skill. Amen."
—*Geoff Rotunno,* **The Boox Review**

"With the edgy wit of Carl Hiaasen, and the detailed, clear description of Raymond Chandler, Christopher Klim takes us on an accurate, fun, and sometimes scary look inside the newsroom of a small city daily newspaper."
—*Bradley Grois, photojournalist* **The Times**

"The interesting characters, hilarious plot, and believable but humorous dialogue keep the readers turning the pages. ... JESUS LIVES IN TRENTON is delightful."
—*Maryanne Raphael,* **Writers World**

Look for the companion book

Write to Publish Handbook

Hopewell Publications, ISBN 0-9726906-9-8

Take your prose and storytelling skills to the next level with focused and entertaining lessons to power creativity and strengthen the essential elements of modern fiction and memoir.

Follow an award-winning author through the crafting process for a story, from idea to finished prose.

WRITE TO PUBLISH

Essentials for the Modern Fiction & Memoir Market

Christopher Klim

Hopewell Publications

Published by Hopewell Publications, LLC
PO Box 11, Titusville, NJ 08560-0011 (609) 818-1049

www.HopePubs.com

Library of Congress Cataloging of Publishing Data
Klim, Christopher, 1962-
    Write to publish : essentials for the modern fiction &
    memoir market / Christopher Klim.
        p. cm.
    Includes bibliographical references and index.
    ISBN 0-9726906-9-7 (pbk. : alk. paper)
    1. Authorship--Marketing. 2. Fiction--Authorship.
    3. Autobiography--Authorship. I. Title.
PN161.K58 2003
808'.02--dc21
                                2003002529

First Edition

Printed in the United States of America

For my wife, Karin, who always believes.
For my mentor, Robert Gover, who knows the way.
For my students who teach me every day.
For readers who want more from a story.
For aspiring writers, who wade through blind alleys and
misinformation, determined to come out the other side.

Thanks to Margaret and Karin for painstaking edits.

Contents

FOREWORD V

I. STORYTELLING IS THE ANSWER..........................1

WHO KILLED THE STORY? 1
SEARCHING FOR STORY 3
A STUDENT OF STORY 5
THE WRITING RITUAL 6
EXERCISES 8

II. ENGAGING OPENINGS 9

ENGAGE, ENGAGE, ENGAGE 10
WHAT IS A NOVEL? 14
EXERCISES 15

III. THE ESSENCE OF CHARACTER 17

SKETCHING CHARACTERS 19
USING THE CHARACTER SKETCHES..............................24
PROFILE THE CHARACTERS 25
LOOKING FOR CHARACTERS 28
EXERCISES 30

IV. SELECTING POINT OF VIEW............................31

WHAT IS POINT OF VIEW?...31
FIRST PERSON 32
SECOND PERSON 33
THIRD PERSON (IN THREE FLAVORS) 35
SELECTING POINT OF VIEW CHARACTERS....................39
EXERCISES 42

ii Contents

V. SETTING THE STORY LANDSCAPE 43

WHEN DOES THE STORY TAKE PLACE? 44
WHERE IS THE STORY LOCATION? 46
WHAT IS LIFE LIKE IN THE STORY? 46
APPLYING SETTING TO THE STORY 47
SETTING IS THE WRITER'S FRIEND 49
RESEARCHING SETTING 50
THE TRUTH ABOUT FICTION 52
EXERCISES 53

VI. PLOTTING FOR CONFLICT AND SUCCESS 55

SEARCHING FOR DRAMA 56
CONFLICT VS. PROBLEMS 58
CONSTRUCTING A STORY 59
STORY ENDINGS 64
SEQUENCING 64
THEME 66
EXERCISES 67

VII. PROFESSIONAL REVISIONS 69

THE FIRST LOOK 70
LEVEL ONE: THE OPENING 71
LEVEL TWO: STRUCTURE/CONTENT 72
LEVEL THREE: STYLE 76
LEVEL FOUR: PRESENTATION 80
EXECUTING REVISIONS 81
SOLICITING FEEDBACK 82
WHEN IS A STORY FINISHED? 83
EXERCISES 84

VIII. THE VIEW TOWARD MANHATTAN 85

A GLIMPSE INSIDE THE IVORY TOWER 86
THE EDITORIAL PIZZA PARTY 87
THE TITLE IS READ FIRST 89
EXERCISES 91

IX. CONNECTING WITH THE INDUSTRY 93

QUERY LETTER 94
SYNOPSIS 96
MANUSCRIPT 97
THE WRITER 98
WHAT IS AN AGENT? 99
LOCATING AGENTS & EDITORS 101
SUBMISSION ETIQUETTE...................................102
BREAKING INTO THE BUSINESS 104
EXERCISES 104

X. SEEKING CREATIVITY 105

SEARCHING FOR STORY IDEAS............................106
WRITER'S BLOCK...108
EXPANDING CREATIVITY 109
WRITE WHAT YOU KNOW 110
FIND YOUR VOICE..110
WRITING SEX SCENES 111
INSPIRATION..112
EXERCISES 113

XI. LIFE SUPPORT 115

REALITY CHECK...115
REJECTION..117
SEEKING HELP 118
FINALLY 118

APPENDIX 121

THE FINAL INGREDIENT 123
CHARACTER SKETCH 139
SCENE & SEQUEL ANALYSIS...............................142
SHORT STORY QUERY LETTER 144
NOVEL QUERY LETTER.....................................145
NOVEL SYNOPSIS 146
SHORT STORY TITLE PAGE & MANUSCRIPT 148

iv Contents

NOVEL TITLE PAGE & MANUSCRIPT 151

BIBLIOGRAPHY, FILM & MUSIC 155

ABOUT THE AUTHOR 157

INDEX 159

Foreword

"Making a book is a craft, like making a clock;
it needs more than native wit to be an author."
– Jean De La Bruyère

Some people believe in the magic of writing. They recognize good stories. They may write, edit, sell, or teach writing and literature. They may talk about voice and dispense intangible rules about structure and form, and while no one perfect approach exists, they often fail to articulate the essential elements of a story. Storytelling involves the craft of writing. It is innate to certain writers but learned by most on the road to success.

The majority of writers demonstrate suitable inspiration, but skilled craftsmanship delivers the possibilities in a salient manner. Talent cannot be taught, but you can learn the basics of story structure and craft. Through discussion, example, and exercise, this book explains the craft of storytelling in the written form and ways for reaching editors, agents, and ultimately, readers in the modern fiction and memoir market.

I. Storytelling is the Answer

*"Any man that does not accept the
condition of human life sells his soul."*
— *Charles Baudelaire*

Storytelling is the oldest art form, dating back to the
Stone Age, before written language. Imagine cavemen around
a campfire. The one who described the hunt in a compelling
fashion probably garnered the most attention. This scenario
has changed little over time. The necessity for a relevant story
remains as vital to humans as food and water. A story forms a
metaphor for life experience, delivered in an infinite variety of
styles, contexts, and mediums. It is how we make sense of the
highs and lows and everything in between. A good story holds
a mirror to our lives. A great story changes our lives.

WHO KILLED THE STORY?

There is a difference between comprehending a story
and writing one, and both require constant practice. At the

conclusion of a story, the reader is satisfied and hopefully enriched, but the primary responsibility of a storyteller is to entertain. A story is not self-serving or wandering prose. Writing is an art form, like music or film. The artist's concept is translated into the medium and reflected back in the reader's head with some semblance of the original design. Readers will not devote their time to a particular piece, unless they are engaged and held in place. If writers want anyone other than their friends to read their words, their stories must entertain.

Some people pronounce the written word as dead. This declaration is the purest form of comedy, founded in a grain of truth yet skewed to the absurd. It is a fact that novels share space with television, film, and even theater, but the written word diverges from all visual media. It takes shape in a reader's mind, with infinite permutations, wrought by a talented author who understands drama and the human condition. A written story is only concrete in the imagination. The skill a writer employs to manipulate the reader's mind defines their talent.

Talent is the soul of writing. It is the art and intangible essence of a story that creates and adds nuance. It cannot be increased or measured, but we can amplify talent by learning about the craft.

Having talent alone is not enough. The road to success is littered with gifted artists who failed to learn the craft of their art form. Great prose writers may hook readers, while exhibiting little or no sense of story. For these writers, the novel is indeed dead, and for their readers, it is a story going nowhere, a fancy room without function. Terrific prose without a story serves few people. Stunning phrases merged with a compelling story wins awards, but the story always comes first. The bestseller list is crowded with workaday prose writers who tell great stories. Clearly, readers desire stories.

SEARCHING FOR STORY

Most writers are storytellers from birth. They construct scenes in their heads, like theatrical plays. They dissect events, searching for the dramatic core. At the start, they aren't thinking about book contracts and publishing deadlines, but they imagine their stories being heard by the public and garnering a reaction.

This is the essential difference between an artist and an artisan. The skilled artisan constructs a fine table or garden, hands over the project, and walks away. He spares no detail and is confident in a job well done. A skilled artist works toward a similar goal, but he must have people appreciate his work. He craves the feedback. He dreams of it.

Writers are lifelong dreamers, pondering events to gain clarity and understanding. We are observers, recording the world around us. It is a quiet interior world and a great place to start learning the craft. Many writers begin storytelling by mimicking the events they recall from television and books or recreating the people they encounter. This is not the habit of an average person.

The behavior of a successful writer promotes an inappropriate set of social skills. He is at times antisocial. A writer requires many hours in solitude, during which he doesn't return phone calls, remember birthdays, or go out in public. When he ventures into daylight, he eavesdrops on conversations for character details and interrogates new and interesting acquaintances.

I can't count the number of times people have said:

"My husband [or wife or girlfriend] claim they had the most interesting conversation with you yesterday." All they did was talk about their lives, and I let it happen. I had asked question after question about their job and life, revealing the interesting facts about their character and circumstance.

Most people don't discuss themselves in significant detail, not even their spouses will listen. Psychiatrists charge $100 per hour for that service. If a writer hangs in long enough and remains interested, he will uncover the unique experiences of any person on the planet. He can use that information.

That is part of a writer's job: interpreting the human condition. It is his ingrained calling to document life. He aspires to achieve an inside vantage point at the height of conflict. As far as the story goes, he doesn't choose sides. He doesn't care who wins or loses. When conflict subsides, he processes the emotion and human cost. He needs to capture it in words.

This is another habit of a working writer. He writes every day, on schedule, regardless of family, illness, or weather. He gives his best hours to the process. This sounds demanding, but a writer can't think of a better way to spend his time. Regardless of his career path, he returns to writing. Even as publisher's rejection slips pile on his desk, he cannot ignore the facts. He feels compelled to write.

My Iroquois ancestors teach that we are given two important questions to answer within our lifetime: Who am I? Why am I here?

In search of answers, writers often take circuitous paths to publishing. Few lucrative opportunities exist for fledgling writers who desire to learn their craft. Many poten-tial authors avoid writing altogether. I went to college for engineering and worked in the space program, only to one day abandon my trade and pursue a career in telling stories. No safety net exists for unknown artists, but I have never regretted my decision to embrace a career in writing. I am not sure where I will end up, but I often recall what Thomas E. Kennedy scribbled in a volume of *Realism and Other Illusions*: "Christopher, May you never need a day job again." Amen to that.

A STUDENT OF STORY

Scores of people desire to be authors. Let's eliminate a large group of aspiring writers right from the start. Many people like the idea of crowded book signings and three-minute spots on morning television shows. Some dream of sumptuous Manhattan lunches with top editors and agents. Others envision movie rights, fat royalty checks, or seeing their book on the shelf beside accomplished authors, bolstered with stunning book reviews blurbs. But not everyone loves writing a book.

Success for a writer is a blessing, but most discover that every minute away from their desk creates a different kind of burden. A writer craves the moment of inspiration and the uncertainty of how it will manifest in a story. Alone in her writing space, she creates entire worlds from imagination. It is the greatest effort she can put forth, not television interviews and book signings.

This career choice might bore a heart surgeon or an NFL quarterback. It might not excite the guy who bags our groceries, but a writer tells stories. If she doesn't, she becomes unsatisfied, unreasonable, and depressed. To ward off these demons, she writes every day. She sets aside a place to work. She establishes a regular schedule. She unhooks the phone and unplugs the television. As John Updike claimed to have done, she deletes solitaire from her computer. She'd rather write than eat.

If writers are compelled to put down words, they are also obsessed with reading. Let's eliminate another large group of aspiring writers. Many aren't avid readers. That is funnier than proclaiming the death of the novel. A person cannot be a meaningful writer, without being a voracious reader. Every art form is built upon that which comes before it. For a start, writers read the type of work that they'd like to emulate. They also read tons of nonfiction as story research, and their book list extends well beyond that. Wandering off a familiar block expands our minds. Writers seize whatever book grabs their attention. If they think a particular piece of writing might perturb or enlighten them, they try it. Only the consuming act of writing interrupts their reading schedule, but if they are not regular readers, I hope they don't waste our time with their written words.

I am harsh on non-readers, but don't worry. They will never pick up this book to be insulted. They don't even hear me. The latest rerun of *Three's Company* or *Gilligan's Island* is blasting too loudly on the television for them to notice.

THE WRITING RITUAL

After committing to a regular writing schedule, create a writer friendly environment. Rent an office or set aside a corner of your home. Make it as plain as possible. A gorgeous view opens beyond my office window, but I positioned the desk so that I can't see it while I am working. I view white walls and a picture of Albert Einstein. (I'll get to him later.) In a bland setting – the kind that should rarely appear in a story – I conjure a mental blank canvas to start constructing and populating an imaginary landscape. I don't know where story ideas are born, but I must lower the mental noise to hear them approaching.

Next, start a ritual. Writing a first draft is part spiritual, that controlled madness from where art and inspiration evolve. Each morning, I spend time reading what I have done the day before, revising the occasional line. I build a running start from which I launch my newest work in continuum of what has gone prior. I am entering the writing zone, like a trance, but wait. Do I know where I am headed? Do I know who is in the story room and what the room looks like? Do I know what everyone is trying to accomplish? Will it be compelling enough for anyone else to care?

Effective stories have a basic framework: engaging openings, at least one empathetic character with a compelling desire, intriguing settings, sustained drama, and a satisfying conclusion. These are the basic precepts of character, setting, and plot. They apply to modern memoir just the same, and I will make the case that they work for in-depth journalism, where the main thrust resembles a biography. It is best to consider each aspect of the framework, before committing a single word. This information, along with research and revision, is the craft of storytelling. Writers spend most of their time here. Developing the patience and determination of a working writer accelerates the learning curve and promotes good stories.

What constitutes a good story? You already know. It is intuitive, but I will reveal the components as best as I can. I will take an analytical approach to content, presentation, and style. I have developed these methods during more than a decade of story crafting and a lifetime of storytelling.

You may apply the techniques in this book to your ideas or manuscripts in progress and obtain immediate results. You may fold only one or two techniques into your story-telling skill set. Most writers have solid story ideas and the desire to take them to the next level.

I cannot guarantee that you will be published and sitting on the Riviera counting the oodles of cash rolling in from your book royalties and film rights. Ah, what a lovely dream that is, but I am sure I can help. I want you to succeed. If you work hard and often, you will notice a difference. I hope that eventually the right editor or agent will unveil your manuscript and announce, "This is a writer who knows what he is doing."

EXERCISES

Envision your short and long term writing goals. Put names to them and build a list. Replace vague desires with concrete goals. Attach proposed dates to your goals. (i.e. finish short story this month, finish novel by year end, query three publishers this week, etc.) If you fall short, forgive yourself and regroup, but remember to reach high. You cannot touch your grandest dreams if you never give them a name.

Work to elevate your skill. Successful people rarely sit tight with accomplishment. They push the bar higher. Don't be afraid to fulfill your deepest desires. If you succeed, you can always ask more of yourself.

II. Engaging Openings

"Look twice before you leap."
— Charlotte Brontë

Television is a good indication of where we are headed in the story form. We are trained to receive the major story elements in the first minute of the program. We immediately know who and what the story is about and where it takes place. A skilled writer makes the best use of the reader's instinct for this information.

Story openings have been likened to a contract with the reader. The framework proposed from the outset builds reader expectations for the ensuing pages. So why not be honest, as much as a storyteller can, and set the stage for your tale from the start. It will go a long way to clarity and the possibility of getting noticed.

ENGAGE, ENGAGE, ENGAGE

Students often ask me how to begin a story, and if they don't, I tell them, "Engage, Engage, Engage." Grab the reader from the start, and I'm not suggesting that you tackle someone in a bookstore, sit on his or her chest, and begin reading from your chapbook of poetry.

This chapter contains a checklist of items to look for in a story opening. These are the essential elements of a healthy story, but don't try to tell the whole story on the first page. The opening entices the reader to turn to the next page and so on. It is a delicate balance. Too much detail bogs down the story progression. Too little information confuses the reader. These are losing scenarios and good reasons to put down the story. When the author poses the right questions, we keep reading to find the answers.

The following sections reveal the elements to consider in a story opening. I introduce each, and describe them in more detail throughout the book.

Introduce the Main Character

The main character is whom the story is about. It is what readers look for first in the story. Try introducing the main character in the starting paragraph, like the opening scene of a movie. When people approach a group of strangers, they seek the most amiable or interesting personalities. We are looking for intrigue. The possibilities range from heroic to downtrodden. We want to be guided to the most compelling soul in the story.

It is the writer's choice to sketch the first impression

of the main character. Have the character demonstrate an element of his personality or the story through action, and unless it is absolutely stunning, avoid long expository paragraphs of physical description and personal history. We will learn those details soon enough, just not all at once and at the lead of the story.

Show the Predominant Point of View

Who is telling the story? This is often the main character, although it doesn't have to be. In *The Great Gatsby*, the story narrates from a friend's perspective. In some stories, we never learn the narrator's name. In others, the narrator is not even in the story; it is an omniscient voice peering down on the world, such as the author himself. In each scene, the point of view is critical to the story. It is how the story is told.

The author may choose to switch the point of view throughout the story, but in most cases, one will dominate. Readers accept this and become comfortable with this vantage point. Try using it in the opening scene, even if it switches during the course of the story.

Reveal the Story Question

Every character has a goal or desire, and the main character's goal is the story question. This goal arrives as a result of internal or external pressure.

As readers identify with the main character, they attach to that character's hopes and dreams. Readers follow characters through the framework of the story, until the story question is resolved in a satisfying fashion. This does not have to be a happy resolution, but it needs to make sense for the character and plot. Nothing cheats readers more than a preposterous conclusion that surfaces at the last moment.

The goal of the main character must be the most compelling in the story. If a secondary character's goal surpasses the main character's goal, it hijacks the storyline. Let's say the story is about Bob's desire to become a professional stock car driver, while his wife battles breast cancer at home. His wife's life and death struggle is more dramatic than Bob's concerns, unless he nearly burns to death in a fiery crash, and that desperate attempt to rescue Bob's story is pathetic.

When a secondary character takes over the story, there are two solutions: extract the secondary character and her goal into their own story, or refocus the story on the secondary character and her goal. The most compelling character in a story cannot be suppressed. Chalk it up to fate. Most writers consider it a gift from the muses. The real story has emerged.

Preview the Setting

Where does the story take place? If it is a Hawaiian locale, begin the story there. The bulk of the story probably occurs in the same or a similar place. Don't fool the reader. Let them see this wonderful and intriguing setting, which only the author can bring to life, right from the start. If this isn't an exciting place on some level, consider another location, although a talented writer can turn a coin operated laundry into a carnival of details.

Create Action

This is truly the point of engagement. In the opening, get the scene moving. People are defined by their words and actions. Instead of stagnant descriptions of setting and character, put the scene in motion, including the people in it. In a movie that takes place on a sailing vessel, do you prefer a thirty second lead-in of the ship sitting at the dock, or one where the sails are billowing in the wind, the hull is cutting water, and the crew is hopping from port to stern? Activate the scene.

Set the Tone

This is the most logical of all. Introduce the story's major tone (i.e. dramatic, humorous, romantic, etc.) at the outset. The tone may shift at times during the novel, but selling one type of story and delivering another is akin to fraud. A dramatic story that turns comic in chapter two, or vice-versa, is really funny but not in a desirable way for the author.

Shorten the Timeline & Establish Order

Begin the story as close to the ending as possible. The increased pace will heighten the drama. Don't feel constrained by real life examples. The writer is the architect of the story. Readers will accept incredible events in a short span of time, if presented in a logical manner. Haven't we all had incredible days or weeks? All stories are a slice of life.

Also, try to keep the story in a straight line. Time occurs in a straight line, at least for now. Readers expect the pace of a story to proceed in fluid increments. Each time the story jumps, even if it is merely forward along the storyline, the narration makes an abrupt shift. If this is a difficult transition, the writer is under pressure to reestablish the storyline. This involves the overall structure of a story or the sequencing of scenes, which is discussed at greater length in the section on plotting.

WHAT IS A NOVEL?

Years ago, I was posed the following question. What is a novel? It was quick and to the point. In the dictionary, novel means unique. A story is a unique collection of words, structure, and ideas. You may avoid the suggestions in this book and still be a successful storyteller. The aforementioned checklist of story elements is only a guideline, and it is certainly not inclusive. There are times when you cannot adhere to the rules either. The annals of literary classics are filled with examples that break the rules and win, but be leery of the pitfalls. Going against the tide is often a master's trick. I hope you are up to that.

When the opening scene concludes, is the reader hooked? That is the magic to which people refer. A writer creates a place that readers want to inhabit. There are people to appreciate, landscapes to explore, and questions to answer. Readers go along for the ride, and the writer is driving.

A skilled writer establishes consistency or suspension of disbelief. He creates a world that readers never question, no matter how fantastical or absurd. Every word builds anticipation toward the conclusion, and inconsistencies or abrupt shifts in the story will grind like the gears of a sticky car transmission. It is another opportunity to lose a reader.

Many writers have compact and concise writing styles, and this translates to their storytelling. The world bustles with activity, and writers can't create more time for readers. In story openings, efficient writers rush to the point, hitting only the highlights needed to get the story rolling. They achieve clarity in a preponderance of words, as opposed to the pound-age of the pages. Smart writers are greedy with words. They try to relate more things in the same space than other writers use for less information. Readers quickly get up to speed and are engaged much faster.

If you accept my advice and include much of what I relate in this book, you will go far in presenting a cogent and fluid story. Hopefully, readers of your particular brand of storytelling will notice and cheer. Then you may dazzle them with groundbreaking new work.

EXERCISES

Go to your bookshelf and pull down your favorite stories. It doesn't matter what you like – fiction, biography, Dr. Seuss. Read the openings. If you remember them well, chances are they are solid stories. They will demonstrate many of the elements mentioned in this chapter. After the first few paragraphs or pages, you will know who the story is about, who is telling the story, and what they want to accomplish, if not a great deal more.

May I suggest a few terrific openings? *The World According to Garp* by John Irving breaks a few rules and succeeds. *A Christmas Carol* by Charles Dickens is a classic, considered the perfect story by many. *Exposure* by Kathryn Harrison is a gripping psychological thriller.

III. The Essence of Character

"Man is a clever animal that behaves like an imbecile."
— Albert Schweitzer

If you grasp Schweitzer's conundrum about mankind, you understand a great deal regarding character. Writers are brave souls. We are downright precocious. We dissect the human condition and attempt to make sense of it. Genuine storytellers translate their findings about humanity into words.

One night as a child, I slept in an adjacent room listening to the adults talk late into the evening. Uncle Joe was an experienced meatpacker, and mom asked him about the difference between calf liver and baby beef liver. Uncle Joe followed with a winding and languorous explanation that never really answered her question, although the endless discourse sounded poignant and funny. Some people might turn frustrated, as mom did at one point, while most enjoyed the ride. But as I lay quietly in my sleeping bag in the next room, I kept forming questions. Why couldn't Uncle Joe answer mom's question? Why did he double-back over meaningless details? Why was it so funny? The short answer is, while Uncle Joe was an eloquent speaker in daylight, it was very late, and he was deep into a bottle of scotch. The long answer is, in my kid brain, I was pulling apart the character named Uncle Joe.

Writers tend to analyze people like that. They size up people's clothes, the way they walk and talk, and the things they do upon entering a room. They probe an individual's upbringing and psyche too. Thank God, everyone doesn't scrutinize to that level. I'd never speak in public again if the audience dissected my personality like a mad psychologist. When I do receive a message critiquing my live performances, guess who it is? It is another writer.

A good story begins with a character. In my mind, characters rule. It is why readers sign up to follow a story. We are human and want to view a little of ourselves in the drama. The main character of a story must garner reader empathy, or the reader will never follow that character through the story, no matter how terrific the plot, no matter how compelling the events thrust upon that character. The reader must first care.

If you think about your favorite stories, you find that the primary characters stick with you. You may forget the settings and most of the plot, but the best characters remain, three dimensional in your mind's eye. You remember how they looked, moved, and reacted to situations. Their actions and emotions resonate for years and possibly forever.

A good character does not have to be a nice guy either. Thomas Harris' Hannibal Lecter is an excellent example. He is brilliant and interesting. He has six fingers on one hand. We are intrigued. We are willing to follow him on his journey, from city to city, from savory meal to savory meal. Sure, he has that one little problem. He likes to eat people, but the author is deft at not turning off the reader. If Hannibal eats a small child or a grandmother, we won't stand for it, and the story comes crashing down. Everyone Hannibal serves on a plate with fava beans had it coming to them. Didn't they?

If the seed of a story begins with an idea or a short series of dramatic events, then a character conveys and amplifies the point. Before going too far along the storyline, pose the following questions. Who is in the story? Who is needed to execute the rough idea of a plot? Who populates the imaginary landscape?

At this point, begin sketching story characters. They will help navigate the plot. They will command the dialogue. With deeper understanding, you will speak with characters in the shower and while driving your car. People will consider you a lunatic, but it is a beautiful day when characters come alive. Good characters will become members of your family.

SKETCHING CHARACTERS

Once you have an idea for a story, try sketching the major characters for clarity. As in real life, a particular person needs to function by their rules. Have you ever done something that, although not particularly bad, doesn't feel right for you? You were acting out of character, operating against your innate sense of who you are in this world. We each carve a unique path in life. The right course for one person may not satisfy another.

Story characters adhere to this same rule. If a character is forced by the author to make uncharacteristic moves, the story will appear phony. It is best to know who is in the story, so we can set the course of the novel in the proper direction.

Characters will go where you want them to go, but they will do it their way. If you uncover their personalities in advance, you can predict their most dramatic moves.

Explore the following categories to help construct salient story characters.

Name

People have names, and so do your story characters. Often, students present manuscripts with uncertain or undefined names. This is an issue of commitment. Once a name is chosen, the particulars of the character become narrowed down. A name suggests ethnic background and even country of origin. It speaks of the character's parents. Names can be powerful. Some have meanings, wrought forth from olden days. Others are new and trendy, as if ripped from the side of a cereal box. I own three books of baby names to consult and cross-reference when choosing character names.

Body Specifics

Story characters possess genetic characteristics that, regardless of the best Hollywood surgeons and trial attorneys, follow them throughout life. These include their age, gender, height, weight, body dimensions, facial structure, hair, and voice. The list of physical details is endless.

Some writers spend a great deal of time here. These are visual aspects, and we are visual people. Body specifics are limiting agents for the character. Age, gender, and body dimensions often define the breadth and depth of capabilities.

Body Language

Psychology begins to enter when we discuss human body dynamics. Scores of books have been written on the subject. How we position our bodies in space reveals our personalities and betrays our inner thoughts.

For the purposes of a story, consider the character at rest and in motion. Does he slouch in a chair? Does he stand erect? Does he cross his legs? Does she glide through a room? Does she limp? Does she wring her hands? Does he twitch his head? The possibilities are endless. Look for interesting and useful details, but don't give every character a strange tick, otherwise it will look like the medication line at a psychiatric hospital.

Presentation

Many of the aforementioned character details are a culmination of fate and circumstance, but the way a character presents himself to the world is a personal decision. Clothing, hairstyle, and speech pattern are cognitive decisions of character. They speak of social status, education, financial inclination, overall preference, and personality type. Look for character-chosen details over the God-given details. The former says a lot more about the character.

Background

Characters don't arrive in a story as fully formed people. They had prior lives. They grew up and experienced certain events. They acquired various skills. As in real life, a character is in large part a culmination of their abilities and experiences. Most writers include little of this information in the story, but it is a good idea to delve into the character's personal history. What led the character to this point in time? What significant events defined them? What did they learn?

Throughout life, we reach critical points of decision that define our course for the future, if not for ourselves as people. We develop skills that aid us along the way. These are our personal background details, and everyone possesses a unique set of skills and experiences that makes sense within the whole person. No person is better, just different.

Psyche

At this point, we have sketched a pretty good character from the outside, poking a finger or two into the interior. Let's ponder two important questions. How does the character view the world, and how does the character place himself in it? This is the moment when I become engaged with a character. My sketch transforms into a real person, as opposed to an imaginary figure to serve my needs. Answering the above questions goes a long way to anticipating a character's reaction to story situations.

Strengths & Weaknesses

Select strengths that will support the resolution of each character's goals and desires, and select weakness that will sabotage their chances of success.

We all have positive and negative traits that govern our personalities. Consider the times you have won. What skills did you employ to outpace your competitors? Ambition? Genius? Stealth? Compassion? Now think of the moments you have lost. How did you blow it? Impatience? Ignorance? Fear? Doubt?

Major traits rule each character, for better or for worse. The right combination prepares a character for growth during the course of the story. A story character is a work in progress like any human being, supported and undermined by life and circumstance. A character may encounter an epiphany near the climax of the story and react in a variety of ways. There is nothing like a good dose of reality to set someone on an emotional tear. If the circumstance contains drama – and a good story reveals plenty of drama – the character involved isn't likely to come through unscathed.

Motivation

When sketching story characters, pass from the physical into the psychological and uncover their motivations. That is the most interesting detail of anyone I meet. Why does an individual behave in a particular way?

Many detectives are trained to ignore morality issues during an investigation. They seek the motivation of a potential suspect or the reason why a criminal behaves in a certain way. The notion of right and wrong is for the prosecutor to evaluate. Guilt is for a judge and jury to decide. A writer is a detective of sorts, and judgment calls are left to the reader.

By uncovering a character's motivation, we not only understand them more fully, we predict their moves and plot an appropriate course for them in a story. When characters enter a room, they begin talking and acting for themselves, as preconceived by the author.

Good characters in motion create surprises for the reader, even for the author. Stephen King claims a story is 'a found thing,' like digging for fossils in the dirt. Good characters reveal amazing discoveries and travel to unforeseen ends.

USING THE CHARACTER SKETCHES

Character sketches are for the writer of the story. Readers prefer to not see every detail that was laid out in advance. They don't seek an explanation of psyche or motivation either. They want the details relevant to the story and will absorb the essence of character as demonstrated by words and actions. In the course of events, a character reveals who they are and why they are here on the planet. Throughout the story, the writer presents evidence of this to the reader.

When applying character details to the story, interject them in proportion to their importance to the story. When the main character stops for a donut, do we need a paragraph description of the girl behind the counter if we never see her again? Each incident summons expectation within the reader. When the writer devotes a lot of time to a particular area, the details flag that story element as being important.

I generally dislike straight narrative prose describing a character. It makes the story stand still.

Jane's right leg ran three inches longer than her left. Pants were out of the question. She wore short skirts, all leg, a little more on one side. In front

> of Bob, she sat down and crossed her legs. He was
> a detail man. She wanted him focused on the report.
> "Take a look at page three," she said.

Try putting the character in motion or conversation, and then embed character description, like drops of water. This fleshes out the character on the fly, with the least amount of narrative noise. It draws us closer to the character, which is where we prefer to experience the story.

> "Good morning, Bob." Jane sat down and
> crossed her legs, surreptitiously holding her skirt
> from riding up her thighs. "I brought the report."
> "Good." Bob gave her the once over. "Let's
> have it."
> She refused to glance down. Her longer
> right leg almost touched the floor, but with her legs
> crossed, no one noticed the difference. "Take a look
> at page three."

The way a character moves, reacts, and speaks defines them in a reader's mind. Some writers claim this is all that is needed. It shows the characters, instead of describing them. It is the difference between watching a movie and reading the screenplay. Writers put their characters on stage.

PROFILE THE CHARACTERS

In the politically correct era – an era that seemed a bit too much like mind control – profiling became a bad word. For the purposes of storytelling, it is a good habit. A writer understands who serves what purpose in the story.

Stories have a protagonist or hero. Sometimes this is an anti-hero like Hannibal Lecter. In any event, we are rooting for him. He is the main character, and we want him to win by solving his story question. In Hannibal's case, it might be filling his stomach with unlucky yet deserving foes.

Stories also have an antagonist, someone or something to thwart the hero. Can you believe someone might want to stop Hannibal Lecter? The nerve! In *The Perfect Storm*, the antagonist is the terrible storm, and by the way, the protagonist's character weaknesses keep him from winning.

If the story has a hero and something trying to stop him, that is enough for classic story structure. Picture cavemen swapping stories around a fire. Caveman Joe searches for fire on the active volcano slope. Caveman Bob hunts the biggest Wooly Mammoth for the cavemen festival. Cavewoman Jane needs rare desert juniper berries to tie-dye her squirrel skin dress. These are noble and dramatic adventures, where one person battles nature or perhaps an evil prehistoric tribesman, yet stories are often crowded landscapes, where additional characters serve secondary roles.

The confidante is an important secondary character. It is a friend to the protagonist – a loving spouse or coworker for example – who serves as a sounding board for the protagonist. This is an excellent opportunity, through point of view and dialogue, to describe the main characters and air their inner thoughts. At all costs, avoid the extended interior monologue or the dreaded mirror scene where the point of view character looks into a reflective surface to relate his physical details.

The foil is another useful character. He is a blind alley or deterrent to success for the protagonist. A foil can be a knowing or an unknowing accomplice to the antagonist. A foil is a powerful character. He messes up life for the hero, and a writer aspires to this anarchy. Sometimes a foil comes on like the antagonist – a red herring – until the real antagonist is revealed. That is a beautiful story twist.

There is generally one protagonist in a story. Even when the story represents a body or race of people, it is helpful to focus on one representative character. The reader wants to root for a real person. In Steinbeck's *The Grape's of Wrath*, Tom Joad represents all dispossessed dust bowl farmers during The Great Depression.

The same holds true for the antagonist. The antagonist humanizes the conflict. Try to choose one main story person, even if the hero battles an entire nation. A common phrase used in all forms of media is 'put a face on it.' Everyone from advertisers to journalists search for one person that exemplifies the main thrust of the piece.

When employing foils and confidantes, the story may include any number necessary to facilitate the plot. Try not to build too many important characters in total. A story should not be a test for memory retention. I walk into a cocktail party, suffer multiple introductions, and can't remember more than three names. Many people have that problem.

Antagonist, protagonist, confidante, and foil are theatrical terms. In theater, everyone has a role on stage. Think of the characters in your story. If they don't serve the story question, try removing them. The scenes will be leaner and more focused on the tale being told.

LOOKING FOR CHARACTERS

You are a character. Well, you are. You are an in-
stance of character traits and personal details, and you have a
lot more to share with the world than you think. You have had
unique experiences. You know certain universal truths about
the world. You have met interesting people. You've probably
seen things that few others have witnessed. No?

A student once claimed that he never did anything
interesting, traveled anywhere intriguing, or met anyone of
note. When I asked what he did for a living, he ashamedly
expressed that he spent his entire career in an animal testing
laboratory. Oh brother, I thought, you are kidding me. That is
a place that most of us haven't experienced. The common and
mundane details of his life might be a Pandora's box of
horrors for the right reader, and you'd better believe that
people would read it and be entertained.

How about the people you meet? Think of those you
love and hate, or those who entice or frighten you. By moving
around the planet, you meet many interesting people. You get
to know a few. Hopefully, you took time to ask a few
questions.

Recall your deepest encounters with people. These
interactions teach you about character and life. When important relationships fall apart, it is best to put aside the blame
and start questioning why you became involved and why it
failed. The emphasis here is on you, not the other person.
While learning about yourself, you will cut to the core of
human nature. As a writer, you can use it all, sharing it with
the rest of us, and by using it all, I mean in bits and pieces.
Sprinkle it into your character sketches. We don't want to
hear your life story as it happened. We really don't. Even in

memoir, we want it dressed up to entertain, not a public bloodletting.

Engaging characters are real, not pretty. They can be gorgeous no doubt, but along with that comes a bucket of less desirable qualities. We have all stood close to pretty, bright, or famous people and come away unimpressed. On that same note, the antagonist needs positive qualities too. This creates emotional conflict for the reader. A well-constructed antagonist is often another person whose desires contradict the protagonist, and the battle gets ugly. Few characters are less enriching than the proverbial white knight and black knight, locked in a battle of principle. These are cardboard cutouts, as stimulating as a political campaign speech.

Still looking for characters? Watch people. Eavesdrop on conversations. Question everyone. Cull newspapers, magazines, and television, searching for the winners and losers in life. The news burgeons with examples. The airwaves are rife with character sketches, and they are each a unique surprise. Remember that we are looking for parts, not a whole person, unless you like getting sued for defamation of character.

As for me, a gut-wrenching legal trial is not an experience that I desire in my bag of tricks. I am a collector of character traits and attributes. I am Dr. Frankenstein, working through the night in my laboratory, constructing people from parts I have encountered and parts I'd like to see in the future. From Uncle Joe to people on television, I saw off their arms and legs and stash them in my mental files.

On Iggy Pop's introspective album *Avenue B*, he discusses how he can't get close to people, because as an artist he uses them up. That strikes the point. Want to get our attention? Examine humanity and tell the truth. Hold a mirror to our lives.

EXERCISES

Take one of your ideas or manuscripts in progress and sketch the characters. Look for trouble areas, places where the characters are too similar, uninteresting, or unnatural. Will the positive and negative traits assist and hinder the story question?

If you don't have a story of your own, find a familiar tale and analyze it. It is a good habit. Notice how the author constructs perfectly flawed human beings to fit the story. The appendix holds a character sketch from the short story, *The Final Ingredient*.

Pick up a book on astrology. Each sign has a unique set of positive and negative traits. Cross any two signs together and come up with an interesting mix of personality traits. Some combinations are contradictory, but they exist in the world, perhaps in your neighbor's house or your place of employment. You can do the same character research with any standard psychological text, where human ego is dissected in detail.

IV. Selecting Point of View

"If only we could pull out our brain and use only our eyes."
— *Pablo Picasso*

A beginning writer simply disregards the story point of view. She writes, shifting back and forth into characters' heads at will. It is dizzying. With the best intentions at heart, the writer has created a sloppy, undisciplined scene. The reader tries to settle into the story from a comfortable vantage point but rattles around inside of it, like a penny in a jar.

WHAT IS POINT OF VIEW?

Point of view identifies who is telling the story. It contains two essential components: the character and the grammatical person. This sounds easy enough, but many new writers find it difficult to maintain consistency within a scene. Even veteran writers slip now and then, although they correct their mistakes during the rewriting process. Writers are rarely commended for executing point of view, but they will be disparaged for failure to establish consistency.

While maintaining point of view is a discipline, understanding it is a different issue. Think of the point of view character as the interpreter of a scene. She is the camera eye and the translator for the characters, settings, and events. The tighter the viewpoint runs to her character, the more the facts are slanted by her personality.

The closeness of the viewpoint directly relates to the grammatical person selected, as does the range of information available to that character. What follows is a brief overview of grammatical person.

FIRST PERSON

First person uses 'I' or 'we' to interpret the scene. It asks the reader to enter the skin of the viewpoint character. The narrative speaks as one individual or a group of common people. First person is very popular and a sign of the times. It is the most voyeuristic. It lets the reader experience how the viewpoint character thinks, feels, and integrates the surrounding story elements. As in real life, reliability of the viewpoint character information directly relates to the integrity of the character.

> I have won the race, squashing my competition. No one stands before me. The crowd cheers. I am king of the world.

In a first person scene, the writer is limited to only what the viewpoint character knows and senses. A first person character cannot comprehend information out of her scope, unless it is openly revealed before the character's eyes. Notice how this passage doesn't work.

> I moved toward the mouth of the alley, as the dark stranger entered from the street. He was hiding a gun. He didn't hate me. He was hired to kill me. He was going to shoot.

Unless the narrator is a psychic or crazy, she can't know much about the stranger coming into the alley. She can't be sure if he is looking for her. If she needs to know these facts, they must be delivered to her in the story sequence or made logical to the reader.

> I moved toward the mouth of the alley, as the dark stranger entered from the street. Was this who they warned me about? He probably didn't hate me. He was hired to kill me. He was going to shoot.

Use of first person creates its own pace. Being so close to someone's thoughts and feelings suggests endless continuity. In a first person passage, the writer tends to account for every moment of time.

SECOND PERSON

Second person employs 'you' to interpret the scene. It allows the writer to enter the reader's skin and manipulate thought, feeling, and emotion. The narrative speaks to us directly. It is intimate, yet it must strike a common chord with a broad base of readers. This makes it difficult to carry off for larger works, and for that reason, it is by far the least used perspective.

Brent Spencer's story, *Are We Not Men?*, is an excellent example of second person usage. He discusses the dissolution of relationships, the tearing apart of the soul, and the reassembly of life, in ways that touch the majority of readers.

To be successful in second person, the writer needs to bridge common thought or universal truths. The writer asks you to believe in the character, so you can be that character.

> It is half past nine, and you're late for work. My God, not today. Everyone will be waiting. You throw your legs over the mattress, half in a daze. You fumble for the alarm.

Some writers offer choices as a means of connecting to the majority. If you agree with one choice, you pass into willing suspension of disbelief and let the author take you along for the ride.

> You know she's leaving when she stops answering the phone on the first ring. She forgets to straighten your tie before dinner. She gathers her sweater from your closet in July.

If the character circumstance is uncommon or aberrant, the writer runs the risk of dislodging readers from the narrative. In second person, Jack the Ripper eviscerating a London prostitute might alienate readers.

> You take hold of her lower intestines, and it slips from your fingers. You need to grab two handfuls at once and pull. A blast of body heat and stink

> kisses your face. Sinews snap like rubber bands.
> "Damn mess!" you curse, ripping her cords free,
> tossing her liver and kidneys aside.

The use of aphorisms is another common technique. It is a tersely phrased statement of truth. Writers often slip into an aphoristic passage of second person to nail down a point.

> The car ahead rode the brake. The woman
> behind us honked her horn like a child. A man
> propped his feet on the dashboard and lit a smoke.
> We were stuck on this godforsaken highway,
> burning enough fuel to heat a small school, yet we
> were going nowhere. You know rush hour.

The final sentence asks you to agree with the first person viewpoint. You become intimate with the driver because of your knowledge of similar experiences. If you have never been in rush hour and cannot imagine how it feels to be stuck in traffic, it is not a problem. The passage is brief, and you continue to read with little disassociation from the narrative.

THIRD PERSON (IN THREE FLAVORS)

Third person uses 'he', 'she', or 'they' to interpret the scene. A writer may not desire first person closeness to the viewpoint character, and the third person offers distance, like a memory or an observation. It operates in a variety of sub-modes, ranging from omniscient to a modified form of first person. Descending the range of third person modes brings us closer to the viewpoint character.

Omniscient

Omniscient point of view is the classic narrative form. It is often referred to as 'the voice of God,' but it is actually the voice of the author, who sometimes thinks he is God. This point of view comments on anything at anytime, because it knows everything. While the problems of first person disappear in third person, so does the intimacy. The reader is removed from the character, observing the story at a distance. It is analytical and difficult to deliver tangible emotion.

In the beginning, when man first put story to paper, the scribe included the main character in the first paragraph. He made sure to clarify point of view and set up the story question. These were things that all lovers of story desired, and the scribe knew this. Other storytellers knew this too. The world waited anxiously for proof in the written word.

The Bible is told in an omniscient point of view. It is merely the facts, as related by the author. In the famous climax to Sodom and Gomorrah, an entire city sinks into the desert, and Lot's wife transforms into a pillar of salt. It is a scene that would make Steven Spielberg spill his coffee over his latest screenplay, but the Bible delivers it in a brief and dry passage.

If I rewrote that famous biblical scene, I'd discard the omniscient voice and get a viewpoint character close to the mayhem. I'd milk it for everything it was worth. Readers need to connect emotionally with characters. They want to get inside and garner the dirty little details of life, love, and madness. This is why the tabloids and talk shows prosper.

Standard

This is the common he/she form of writing. The reader views the world through the eyes of a character without the intrepid intimacy of first person. It is observational, like standard journalism. It offers a level of detachment, yet stays close enough to make it real. It offers the opportunity to include tangential information that cannot be reached in first person.

> Jane revved her motorcycle over one hundred miles per hour. The spokes flashed in the moonlight, like money dropping from a slot machine. The road ahead stretched from L.A. to Vegas with barely a cop. Truckers called it the midnight expressway. It'd been a drag strip since the day they laid down the blacktop, but now two cherry tops flashed in Jane's mirrors.

In standard third person, the author's voice is still evident. There is a presentation of information, not specifically interpreted by the character. Humorists and other expert stylists employ this form, interjecting unique observations into the flow, but maintaining an essence of character. The reader is close to the character but not too close, while absorbing the peripheral view with much pleasure.

Third Person Singular

Third person singular (TPS) is a hybrid of first and third persons. It includes the personal experience of first person, but reserves a third person level of detachment in unsympathetic situations. First person closeness is not always desirable, and TPS solves the problem. It is the best of both worlds, requiring the writer to maintain a particular discipline. If it is done well, the writer can grasp every major cognitive and emotional highlight of the scene, while increasing the pace as needed.

TPS appears like pure third person, yet it is bound to the rules of first person. Information cannot be included unless it is known or revealed to the viewpoint character. The reader sees the world through the viewpoint character's eyes, like in first person, as opposed to seeing it through the author's eyes, as in standard third person.

Every line in TPS can be translated directly to first person. That is the proof to see if TPS is working.

Observe the following passage.

> He was long and lanky. He didn't look his best in regular cut shirts and cheap solid ties. He resembled a stockbroker who hadn't done well that year.

Read the same passage translated in first person.

> I was long and lanky. I didn't look my best in regular cut shirts and cheap solid ties. I resembled a stockbroker who hadn't done well that year.

The passage fails. It is mirror writing; the character seems as if he is gazing into a mirror. He perceives himself in ways that sound unnatural. It is hackneyed and to be avoided at all costs. None of the sentences are great, but the first is the worst violation.

Let's rewrite the same passage using third person singular point of view.

> He struggled fitting his long arms and legs into the off-the-rack suit. Forget the cheap solid ties. He didn't want people thinking he hadn't done well that year.

If we translated the passage to first person, it passes the test for TPS. It sounds natural.

> I struggled fitting my long arms and legs into the off-the-rack suit. Forget the cheap solid ties. I didn't want people thinking I hadn't done well that year.

The view is now a character perception. We hear the narration through the character, not the author. We are feeling it too, which supports much needed character empathy.

SELECTING POINT OF VIEW CHARACTERS

While the grammatical person defines the distance and capabilities of a scene's perspective, the viewpoint character, including an omniscient author, interprets the action and ultimately taints the facts through personality.

If you and I hopped in my car and smashed into another car at the first intersection, we'd tell a different version of the events. Why? We are unique people in the world. We speak differently, and we have had different experiences. I may be in several car accidents every year, and if no one was injured, I'd have an indifferent attitude about another fender-bender in a long line of bad driving. Meanwhile, you may have another interpretation of the facts. You may be shocked and barely able to utter a coherent word. Incidentally, this is akin to the first person point of view. We both experienced the action up close, but in the story version, just one of us will talk about it. The choice between you and me changes how the story is told.

If we had witnessed the same car accident from the corner, it is akin to the third person point of view. Again, our previous experiences will color the interpretation of events. If no one was injured and the police were handling the clean up, I may be anxious to leave. I wouldn't care anymore. You may need a stiff drink to calm down. My Lord, that was much too close for you. See the difference? Know your point of view character. They are going to change the way the story is told and ultimately the way readers feel about what happens.

Christopher tugs your shirtsleeve. "Come on, let's leave."

"Did you see that?" you say.

"See what?"

"The car." Your heart pounds. Your throat burns like a discharged gun barrel. You'd been screaming at a total stranger to get out of the way. "We almost got hit!"

"It was ten feet from the curb."

"It darn near went up the sidewalk."

"Everyone's fine. Even the guy on the bike is okay."

"I guess so." You brush the perspiration from your temples, and it is December. "I need a drink."

"Come on. I know a place on 2nd Street."

Which point of view is right for your story? It depends on the type of story and the time period, among other factors. A wide range of flexibility is acceptable. The more a reader identifies with a particular character, the more closely the viewpoint can be tied to him or her, although stunning exceptions always arise. I have culled many essays on the subject and found nothing against experimenting with any combination of character and grammatical person.

Think of viewpoint as selecting a seat for a theater or sporting event. Who in the story owns the best seat in the house to interpret the action? It is not always the closest seat or one particular seat. Switching the seat changes the view and amplifies different aspects of the story, while reducing others.

Try to stay with one point of view per scene. Switching point of view within a scene is a master's trick. When it is done well, it is done brilliantly, but if the writer makes a clumsy transition, it is another excuse for the reader to put down the story.

The same holds true for changing the grammatical person of a viewpoint character. Again, master writers have switched from first to third and vice-versa for the same character, even within a single scene. It is the writer's version of a high wire act, but as with any breathtaking attempt at crafting a story, ask questions. Do you have to do this? Can it be done more simply? If it can, shoot for easy reader interpretation. Writing in the most straightforward and clear manner brings as many of us into the story as possible.

Including multiple points of view within a story is fine, and sometimes it is necessary. Readers want to settle into a story from a few comfortable vantage points. Try to use just one, although it can't always be done. When two viewpoint characters enter a scene, the writer decides who gets the focus. Side with the more important character, although at times it is nice to view a major character from an outside perspective.

Point of view relies on the writer to mix character and grammatical person in the proper proportions. When a story is complete, it merits on the writer's decisions and discipline more than the prose itself. Don't get caught in the fine writing trap. The story always comes first. A reader asks: whose story is it (i.e. character), and how it will be told (i.e. point of view)? All that remains is a question of where the story is headed, and that is a combination of setting and plot.

EXERCISES

There are two primary ways to learn point of view: examine accomplished writers in action through their work, and practice it for yourself. Mock up a basic character and story situation and then select a point of view (i.e. first, second, third person omniscient, etc.). Second person is the most challenging. Most of us rarely write in second person, and the writer must strike universal grains of truth for it to work. I use aphorisms throughout this book. I am speaking to writers, and there are things that we all understand.

Try placing the same character in each grammatical person and observe the difference. Notice how switching the grammatical person modifies the range and texture of the prose. It runs the gamut from intimate to abstract. See what works for the characters in your story, and have fun. If you don't have a story on hand, try changing the grammatical person of a favorite story.

V. Setting the Story Landscape

"I have been a stranger in a strange land."
– Moses

Setting is the most overlooked aspect of storytelling for emerging writers, and many writing manuals never discuss it. Setting is where the story takes place. It offers intriguing details and adds depth and dimension. Setting is a friend to the writer. It works with the devised character and plot. It can add drama and pull the writer out of trouble.

Writers aim to avoid 'white room' syndrome, when the reader has little idea where a particular scene commences. Setting paints the landscape for the reader, and it is found in the details.

An important aspect of delivering story details involves research. While the research process is discussed later, let's begin investigating the basic questions of setting: when, where, and what?

WHEN DOES THE STORY TAKE PLACE?

A story spans a particular time period. Booksellers like to classify stories as historical, contemporary, and futuristic. This is nothing more than past, present, and future respectively, and each changes the parameters of setting. Let's take a closer look at each category.

The Past

The past is recorded in the annals of history. The writer connects with this information through personal experience, experts, and documentation. While expert sources are good, our own memory of the past is unreliable and needs to be verified. We often don't remember things exactly as they were, even once familiar details. We also romanticize the past. Hanging clothes on the line, piece by piece, on a warm spring afternoon sounds sweet, but it was never as nice as shoving them in the dryer. Most writers would rather read a chapter in a book, with the dryer whirling in the background, than work the clothesline.

Another aspect of the past involves historical events. Consider history in two ways: as a backdrop or as an immediate surrounding. In the opening to *The World According to Garp*, World War II is a backdrop. It fills the air with tension, although the specifics of war never enter the picture. In the film, *Tora! Tora! Tora!*, the attack on Pearl Harbor takes over the story. If a story gets close to a major historical event, it is difficult to avoid incorporating that event into the story. It might even take over the story.

The Present

A story in current times includes the tangible past and future. The writer is not redesigning the world but employing it for dramatic effect. Regardless, intriguing locations exist in present times: a peek inside surgery, life on an oil drilling platform, or the machinations of a textile factory in China. Most people haven't viewed these locations up close, but each of us has witnessed unique settings and might make use of them in our writing.

The Future

Fifty years ago, we were projected to be commuting to the space wheel in the sky, with a four-day workweek and loads of playtime for interesting new social games. It appears that the experts guessed wrong about our future. By all accounts, the coming years will be dirtier, noisier, and more crowded, if not busier. This is what made the movie *Blade Runner* so special, besides the twisted ending.

The future is open to interpretation, but whatever world is designed for a story, it must be a logical extension of its own history. Your story world, no matter how absurd, must be justified. If everyone is green-skinned, that needs to be explained in a rational manner. If the planet O consists of orange marmalade, life on the surface must make sense to the reader.

The *Dune* series created its own genre, and it bears an elaborate and interconnecting history. A lexicon is printed on the back pages of the book. The author left no details to chance, and to his many readers, Frank Herbert's world is real.

WHERE IS THE STORY LOCATION?

Story scenes occur in one or more locations. These are physical locations on the planet or in the imaginary world of the writer, although placement is not the only consideration of setting location. A story focus varies from a wide to a tight view. One writer may traverse the global landscape in pursuit of a story, while another remains in the same room for the duration. In either case, writers exploit the setting at hand, seeking the extraordinary details, and much like character details, even the most mundane parts achieve intrigue and brilliance beneath the right light.

WHAT IS LIFE LIKE IN THE STORY?

This is a broad question, involving many aspects of life at a particular location and moment in time. A writer considers food, clothing, transportation, education, occupation, religion, and language, and the list of possibilities is much larger. Any social behavior or lifestyle element may be useful to the story.

Shifting the location offers diverse possibilities. The Pennsylvania Amish live differently than people fifty miles away in downtown Philadelphia. Hawaiians conduct life differently than Alaskans. Each is aware of the other, yet remains bound to the customs and circumstances of geography and culture.

APPLYING SETTING TO THE STORY

Using setting details is a lot like using character details. Apply them in proportion to their importance and impact to the story. Every word that appears in the text garners attention. If the writer embellishes a particular aspect, the reader will assume it to be important. Violating this expectation suffers willing suspension of disbelief, and the reader won't know what to follow in the story.

Seek interesting details, over the common or mundane. In a present day setting, everyone has a good idea how a steaming coffee mug looks, smells, and feels. If the writer offers too much detail, she might run the risk of alienating readers who don't experience coffee exactly that way. Just put the warm mug on the table or in the character's hands, and let the reader fill in the blanks.

On the other hand, the same cup of coffee assumes a new dimension in another time period. In 1776, coffee might take thirty minutes to prepare, while in 2220, coffee might enter your hydration tube at the mere thought of it.

Employ characters to interpret the setting in their thoughts and words, rather than straightforward narrative passages. The story will perform double duty, fleshing out the characters and surroundings at the same time. The opening to Richard Marius' *After the War* simultaneously introduces the main character and landscape via the character's thoughts. In effect, the landscape reflects the character's mindset.

Here is another example:

Bob decided he hated *Danny's*. He loathed the cheap furniture and paper napkins. The blasting music deafened the conversation, and the smell of the kitchen turned his stomach. He might buy the place and plow it under. He couldn't believe he'd married a woman who didn't notice greasy forks, bad service, and stale rolls. Had she always been like this?

If the story must include pure descriptions in the narrative, try embedding them inside dialogue. The landscape will be built without the reader hearing your construction noises in the background.

"This place stinks," Bob said before the waiter arrived. "I'm sorry we came here."

"You picked *Danny's*." His wife was barely audible over the blasting music. Flakes from the old rolls littered the tablecloth. "I thought you wanted to come here."

"It's your favorite place, not mine."

"What's wrong?"

Bob watched the waiter dispense the flatware from his back pocket and leave without pouring water into the glasses. He picked up a fork and scraped his thumbnail over the scabby tines. "Look at this."

"Look at what?"

"The fork isn't clean."

"You never cared before."

"Well, I do now."

When incorporating setting into a scene, try to include all of the senses. We are visual people. Most of us absorb life with our eyes, followed by our ears and nose. Along with sight, sound, and smell, remember to include touch and taste. These senses become more poignant in a well-crafted story.

SETTING IS THE WRITER'S FRIEND

Setting offers an opportunity to manipulate the scene. Employ setting to manufacture drama, by taking ordinary but essential dialogue and placing the characters in an interesting location. While being teased by the action, the reader learns important information about the story.

The following dialogue might be a dull conversation inside corporate headquarters, but moving it increases the impact.

Bob tossed the tennis ball in the air to serve and sent it downcourt. Tom volleyed, and as usual, Bob barely reached the ball, firing it into the fence.

"That's twenty all." Tom shifted side to side.

Bob dug in his pocket for another ball, blinking from the sun in his eyes. "I've been going over the books."

"That's why I pay you."

Bob faulted the next serve. "The numbers don't look good." He took a simple swat at the ball.

"I know." Tom volleyed the return at Bob's backhand.

Bob sent it wildly out of bounds. He stared at the fuzzy yellow ball as it pattered to a halt.

"Twenty-thirty." Tom grinned.

Bob grabbed the ball and returned to the baseline. "The numbers are bad."

"I guess I can't expand this year."

"It's worse than that."

Tom stopped shifting. "How bad?"

"Your company's a shell. It's been completely hollowed out." Bob smashed the ball up the centerline. Ace.

The setting can facilitate entrances and exits to scenes. In the preceding passage, neither the conversation nor the action was finished, yet the scene had hit its climax. The reader learns that Tom's company has been looted. Bob's last serve – an ace – creates an opportunity to nail down the point and exit the scene.

The list of possible setting devices and uses is endless. A writer's goal is to amplify the tension and entertain the reader. As long as the sequence is logical and the characters remain true to themselves, the reader is further enriched by the story, but if the story must continually resort to setting in order to amply the tension, the story may not contain enough drama to stand on its own. Setting helps. It won't cure all.

RESEARCHING SETTING

Research is the real work of setting, journalism, and any writing that requires factual verification. Lazy writers get caught with their pants down, and we have witnessed high profile embarrassments in the news. As for me, I'd prefer to be in the newspapers at the top of the bestseller list.

Be a hero of the reference section. Libraries, bookstores, and a writer's own bookshelf burgeon with reference material. Americans take for granted the wealth of free information at their fingertips.

Be an information junkie. Spend time going over facts, figures, and discourses. If a topic interests you, track it down and do more research. Soon, you might be able to debate the public opinion of the death penalty or know the various breakthroughs in heart treatments. The list of topics is endless, and most can be incorporated into a story. An entire story might even fall out of an encyclopedia passage, magazine article, or travel brochure. At the very least, you can annoy friends, who insist that the tangential facts you produce in conversation are bogus. There is nothing like stopping a debate cold with a verbal pie chart of geopolitical data. Really, it is a very neat trick.

Possible resources for setting exist everywhere. At the moment, writers are tripping over great ideas. Television, radio, magazines, and newspapers span the globe, interviewing key people and highlighting interesting careers and lifestyles. Intriguing material arrives in the mail every day. Personal contacts, including acquaintances and friends of friends, hold vital information or paths to that information. If it is important enough, be willing to intrude. Identify the source, and track it down; just don't do anything illegal. Ask questions.

Remember to record the facts. A writer travels with a pen. When important story ideas and information arise, he scribbles it in a notebook or on the back of a cocktail napkin. He rips articles from magazines or newspapers. He readies a tape for the VCR. He files everything for later use. Breakthrough ideas strike at odd moments. Part of the design for splitting the first atom was scribbled on a restaurant tablecloth, and Einstein and Oppenheimer needed to beg the owner to take it with them.

The Internet is a great resource for information. It allows easy access to most local newspapers, chambers of commerce, tourism bureaus, and community groups. These connections may lead to e-mail conversations with useful people, and that is only the beginning. Writers Notes at www.WritersNotes.com collects useful and free information websites. Writers connect with online reference volumes, search engines, publishing and print industry information, expert sources, various freelance opportunities, and writer's forums, and the list grows with the world wide web.

As with any information, be a journalist and double check all sources. A neighbor may swear that she is the world's leading authority on Amazon tribal migration, but corroborate her stories with another source. The Internet is the worse offender of data integrity. Anyone with a domain name can hang a shingle as an expert. The ex-NASA flyboy on the web might be the acne-faced teenage son of the guy down the block. Verify information and sources.

Learn from the work of other writers. Like a jazz song or a painting, all art is an extension of what came prior. Study the masters and your favorite authors, especially those who write stories like yours. See how they handle settings similar to yours.

Lastly, remember to search yourself for new ideas. Perhaps you held an interesting job or visited unique places. You might have worked at a fish cannery or visited a remote island nation. Common and familiar information to you might be intriguing to the average person. Take us there. Show us what it is like to inspect the production line, as roaring machines spew out thousands of kipper cans per hour. Guide us through the flooded streets of Bangladesh during the monsoons. Light our imagination with the details.

THE TRUTH ABOUT FICTION

An unwritten code exists among writers to get the information correct in the story. This holds true for purveyors of fiction. A particular story might be the only place where people are exposed to a topic of information. It doesn't need to become a learning experience. Chances are that only bits of information will be included to flavor the scene, but if a story includes facts on any known subject, they must be true, not made up to suit the story or mask the writer's inability to perform research.

When I needed to write a scene around a skin grafting operation, I spoke to doctors and read medical journals, but I just didn't have the feel for it. I visited the NY Public Library photo archives and spent the afternoon perusing hideous color blowups of medical procedures. I skipped lunch that day, but I understood the visceral nature of applying various types of skin grafts. I had what I needed to electrify the scene.

Learn to gather the facts for your stories. If you make an educated guess, most readers will never notice, but once an expert reads your story, you will be discredited, if only on a very small scale. You can't afford that. Every written word that you submit to the public builds your reputation.

EXERCISES

Think about your day as you go about dressing, eating, working, cleaning, and sleeping. Consider every aspect of living, recording the mundane and the extraordinary. Now, move your setting to another place or time. Notice which aspects disappear and which become more complex.

Select a topic of interest and go about researching it. Probe the library, bookstores, and Internet. Introduce yourself to the reference librarian at your local branch. Seek experts and industry contacts. See where it leads. If you dig long enough in one area, you will mine an incredible story idea. It's worth the effort.

On your next trip, drop into common places, such as supermarkets, public parks, and restaurants. Watch the people. See how they do similar things as you, yet modified to suit their customs and manners. Notice the surroundings. Aspects of architecture, function, and protocol may seem absurd at first glance but are logical in historical context of the particular location.

VI. Plotting for Conflict and Success

*"The whole object of travel is not to set
foot on foreign land; it is at last to set foot
on one's own country as a foreign land."*
                    – G.K. Chesterton

The act of plotting a story is much maligned, but the notion of plotting as being uninspired is absolutely bankrupt. Some writers claim they never plot and that this separates them as true artists, but then how does drama arise in a story? By itself?

All writers create characters, settings, and events, and in the process, the primary elements of drama are set in place by the author. What once seemed spontaneous and random is firmly under the writer's control. At closer scrutiny, it appears that every writer conceives their plots, some more actively than others. As for the writer who claims not to orchestrate his stories, it suffices to say that a crowd and a cocktail turn most artists into savants. In the end, plots are crafted to perfection.

Plotting is having clues about the journey. It is stepping out the door and knowing the roads required to get to the destination. There are many ways to reach the same destination. Some are scenic. Others are harrowing, but if it is a memorable trip, the destination has purpose. In a story, purpose emanates from the characters. The path selected is a product of their abilities and desires. It is their trip. They decide.

A story journey begins when a character asks: what do I want? Born out of internal or external pressures, it is the genesis of hope and desire. It is the bridge from that first ancient question: who am I? Crossing that bridge poses the second ancient question: why am I here? Good story people take a stab at these questions. There is beauty and drama in the success and failure of answering them.

At this point, it should be obvious why the main character and the story question are presented as early as possible. When mated properly, the story gets rolling but not until then. Readers seek the desire of the main character and prepare for the trials and tribulations of satisfying it. When it is obscured by fuzzy plot direction or too much background information, the story is regarded as going nowhere or wandering. Those are apt descriptions.

SEARCHING FOR DRAMA

My target reader searches for drama in a story. She is unconcerned with character sketches, setting research, and story plotting. When it all comes together, she is intrigued by a character and his goal. My reader comes along for the ride, and sustained drama during the course of the story keeps her glued to the pages. In other words, if the story question is the reason why she begins a novel, drama is why she finishes it.

Without drama, she becomes bored, no matter how brilliant the prose. Her attention wanders to another story, not mine, and I can't let that happen.

What is drama? To paraphrase Alfred Hitchcock, drama is life without the boring bits. He understood drama. Did you ever see a boring Hitchcock movie? He sketched storyboards – sequential depictions of characters in action. He left nothing to chance, maintaining an eye on the dramatic core of each scene. Some accuse Hitchcock of being calculating and manipulative. Yes indeed, and we thank him for it.

In a story, drama is conflict for empathetic characters, hopefully for the main character. Don't worry about messing up life for your story people. Readers prefer happy endings but not happy stories. They want to cry and scream over the journey. They also want to laugh, but sustained satisfaction in a storyline kills the drama faster than a corporate officer collecting stock options.

John Irving once admitted to seeing a woman reading his latest novel on an airplane. She started turning the pages harder and harder, becoming increasingly annoyed, until she slammed the book shut and shoved it in the seat pocket in front of her. Irving was struck by her response. He wondered what was so good to garner a reaction like that. He had experienced a writer's nirvana. He witnessed his drama in action.

To build drama, a writer searches for conflict in every scene. It resonates through the characters, the story, and ultimately the reader. Great stories supply increasing conflict, en route to the climax. The reader clings to the pages, hurtling toward the conclusion. This is nirvana for my target reader.

CONFLICT VS. PROBLEMS

Some writers bog down their characters with problems, yet the story holds little drama. Problems are annoyances and hindrances beset upon the character. They are complications or situations to be solved, but they present no urgency, doing little to increase the tension in the story. Does a flat tire or chipped tooth create a gripping scene? Not typically, but they might inspire drama in the right circumstance. Problems provide methods for conflict, but conflict is a different animal.

Conflict is disharmony between diametrically opposed parties. It doesn't need to be a physical confrontation. It is demonstrated in negotiations, arguments, deceptions, lies, wrong decisions, and opposing needs. It may be internal or external. Conflict arises when desires cross paths. It doesn't have to be good battling evil. Two characters might have different goals, and as their paths collide, serious consequences result. Bob may love Jane, while realizing he must undermine her in order to achieve his most cherished goal. This is internal and external conflict working together to create drama.

Characters have strong points that help resolve their story question, and they have fatal flaws that sabotage their chances at success. This conflict creates a myriad of possible paths to roam within a story. When designing a scene, consider ways to send characters on the most logical and worst path. If a reader worries that the character is headed for disaster, you have put in a good day's work as a writer.

CONSTRUCTING A STORY

A story, especially a novel, is a daunting affair. It is a marathon, not a sprint. The entire path to publishing is a longer marathon, and a novel or short work is another step in the writer's effort to reach the public. Most writers find the trip challenging, with memorable highs and lows, but it is important to see the immediate road ahead, as well as the overall goal. A writer can only conquer the road ahead. This helps maintain focus, if not his or her sanity.

Plotting keeps the writer focused on the short road ahead. Some writers map an entire story journey before they start. Others map only the scene in progress. In the first scenario, the trip itinerary changes as the writer witnesses the characters in action. In the latter scenario, the writer entertains many more rewrites, because the entire journey is never considered until the trip is finished.

Writers will debate the strengths of their approach until breathless, and like many writers, I have covered both extremes of plotting. I prefer to map the journey before I start, leaving every scene open to interpretation as I proceed. For a novel, I design an outline of five to ten pages, including a brief paragraph for each proposed scene. By the time I reach a particular scene, it may be used as planned, expanded into more scenes, or deleted altogether. It depends on the importance of the moment, and I can't know for certain until I reach that point in the journey. It only takes form when I arrive. As I travel, I am focused on the short stretch of story ahead, because I have broken it down ahead of time.

It is widely understood that all stories can be broken down into a series of scenes and sequels. A scene is a self-contained stretch of story drama, and a sequel is a moment of reflection, based on the previous drama. They form the building blocks of a story, occurring in logical sequence along the story timeline. Theoretically, a sequel follows every scene, whether it actually appears in the finished story or not.

When constructing a scene or sequel, try viewing it as a sketch of real life. Its validity should be obvious to the reader. If it is not, it will appear more than obvious. It will be unbearable.

The following discussion is a combination of techniques that merged from years of sketching scenes and sequels. These methods reflect a common idea, although credit belongs to master writers Lawrence Block and Jack Bickham for clarity on the subject.

Scene

A scene is the basic unit of a story. It is one step in the journey. It can expand over multiple chapters, or more than one scene can exist within a chapter, but a scene is easily removed from the entire storyline and analyzed for its merits.

As Hitchcock asserted, scenes are the most important steps in the journey. If Bob wants X, he probably needs to accomplish steps A, B, and C to obtain X. Some writers rush forward to step C and miss the presumed drama in steps A and B. They actually skip the story. Other writers wander to steps D and E, which might not belong in the storyline.

Each scene must serve the overall story. It poses a sub-question to the larger story question. It continues the storyline and hopefully worsens the outlook for the main character. It also raises the tension in the story. In short, it progresses the story question, while increasing the drama. If it doesn't, consider removing it.

When creating a scene, locate its dramatic core. The main character is trying to accomplish something and suffering opposition. If a story has an arc, a scene reveals a smaller arc. The moment is dressed with character and setting details, but this ancillary information is not the entire point of the scene.

To undercover the dramatic core of a scene, there are four basic questions:

What is the objective? The main character in the scene is trying to accomplish something. This is a sub-goal of the character's greater story desire. Answering this question gives the scene focus, not to mention an agenda.

What is the problem? A known complication hinders the objective. This may be a personal flaw or problem developed in the storyline, but the character cannot reach his objective, unless the character acts upon the problem.

Where is the conflict? A person or thing threatens resolution of the objective. While solving the problem, the character encounters dramatic opposition from another source, thereby threatening a positive outcome.

What is the outcome? At the climax of the scene, the character's objective is answered in some fashion. The answer progresses the storyline and changes the character's mental, emotional, or physical state.

Consider this example. Cindy is looking for a new job, when she suddenly gets a lunchtime interview with another company. Her *objective* is to sneak out to the interview and return without her current employer knowing. The *problem* is that Cindy needs to copy her resume, and the office copy machine is her only option. *Conflict* arises when Cindy's boss stops beside the copier and starts asking questions about work. Finally, the *outcome* isn't very good when the boss notices Cindy's resume. No hand-to-hand battle ensued, but Cindy's situation offers a great deal of potential drama, not to mention dire consequences.

Writers will debate whether the outcome to a scene needs to be negative or disastrous. Lousy outcomes add drama by making the situation worse for the main character. Conversely, too many positive returns for the main character stifle the drama. Jack Bickham has stated that the result of the objective should never be purely *yes* or *no*. It is better as *yes, but* or *no, and*. Therein lies the gray areas of life, which skew the facts and create tension.

When building scenes, be flexible. As the writer gains experience with a particular character, he understands the character's abilities in greater detail. Earlier decisions for a character may no longer be valid, and characters forced into plot decisions appear phony to the reader. This is the biggest reason why plots must adapt to characterization. A character will show the writer how to proceed along a storyline. People will do things their way and only their way.

Sequel

A sequel appears after a scene. It is an opportunity for the character to digest the previous action. There are three major aspects of a sequel:

Cognition: what does the character think about the previous scene? This is the character's perception of the recent events.

Emotion: how does the character feel about the previous events? This is the emotional response.

Decision: what will the character do next? The character brings sense and reasoning together to make a decision.

In the previous example, Cindy *perceives* that she is in trouble with her boss. She *feels* angry, scared, and depressed. She *decides* that her current job may be in jeopardy and needs to make the best of the upcoming interview.

Sequels by nature are not progressive along the storyline. They tend to make the action stand still. Most writers work to reduce or remove sequels wherever possible. They are not always necessary. A character's action in their next scene often implies the important aspects of a sequel. Sometimes not knowing a character's response to the action adds drama.

Try reducing sequels to a few short lines or even a single sentence, reserving the lengthier passages for critical moments of change. Some writers embed sequel identifiers en route to the scene's climax. In this way, a character's cognitive and emotional states are spelled out by the end of the scene. As always, employ dialogue. Nothing reflects a character's state of mind like a few searing words.

Using the Scene and Sequel Method

The scene and sequel method is a tool. When a writer approaches a scene, he considers who is in the scene, what they are trying to accomplish, where the scene takes place, where it fits on the storyline, where lies the dramatic core, and how everything will end up. The scene sketching method above assists the understanding process. Employ the method when stuck in a scene that lacks drama. The pointed questions will expose a scene's particular weaknesses.

The appendix presents the scenes and sequels for the short story *The Final Ingredient*.

STORY ENDINGS

On the story journey, it is difficult to know precisely what the destination might look like in advance. We have all seen pictures of the Grand Canyon, but it is another event to reach Mather Point and witness the changing bands of the canyon walls at sunset. Grand Canyon is the destination, and everything we know, hear, and hope surfaces along the journey, but it only takes shape when we arrive.

Author Robert Gover suggests that writers build a container bin for possible outcomes. It holds answers to the story question, and when the writer reaches the climax, he or she will recognize the correct answer for the story.

A story ending needs to resolve the story question in a satisfying fashion. This is not necessarily a happy ending but a logical outgrowth of the story events. Surprise endings are fine, but preposterous results are ridiculous to the reader. If the ending is bleak, add solace or hope for the reader to achieve a certain level of satisfaction.

SEQUENCING

Sequencing involves the order in which the scenes are presented. It refers to the overall structure of the story. One may write an entire manual on story structure. Whether the scenes are presented in chronological or nonlinear order, look for three things: rhythm, transition, and escalation.

Rhythm: If the story intends to skip around in time or point of view, the mind searches for a comfortable pattern. There is a pacing or rhythm to every novel. Establish it from the outset and be rewarded with greater flexibility within the prose. This also applies to switching points of view. After a while, the reader will anticipate a change to another point of view or place in the story timeline. The story has a rhythm.

Transition: Smooth transitions from scene to scene, or paragraph to paragraph for that matter, add to the fluidity of the prose. When reading draft work, it is often clear when an introductory phrase or sentence is needed to smooth a rough transition. Sometimes a hard jump adds drama to a particular sequence. See what works for the scene and story. The transitions in the film *Twelve Monkeys* are maddening, but they work. The story is about time travel. We are not supposed to feel comfortable. The superb novel, *Fight Club*, opens very close to the end. It teases us with the dramatic conclusion, and then jumps back to propel the reader forward to the climax.

Escalation: Whether the scenes appear in chronological order or not, readers seek escalating conflict throughout the story. Gripping stories build drama to the climax. Certain novelists number their scenes and reorder them for heightening drama. Try to accomplish this on a linear timeline, while using flashbacks as brief divergences to enrich the story. If you need to hop around in time, work toward the best rhythm, transition, and conflict escalation possible.

THEME

Theme represents the author's interpretation of life, as dramatized by the story. It is demonstrated through character, setting, objects, actions, tone, commonly held beliefs, or any device that symbolizes the overall message of the story. The title often suggests the theme. After character, theme is the next important item that a reader takes away from the story, but it is not a lecture aimed at readers. It is what the characters experience and learn, and it is closely tied to character change or a character's inability to change. Readers may not be able to articulate the theme, yet fully enjoy the story.

Many writers don't envision theme while drafting their work. The behaviors and symbols relating to theme are added and fortified as the work is revised. This was the case with my first novel. Early readers recognized it as an allegory about man's thirst for grace, and while I subconsciously knew this and set the story in that direction, I never designed it for that effect.

Theme is also interpretive. One reader may reach a different conclusion than another. To a lesser extent, my first novel was a discussion about the adult lives of abandoned children. This really struck some readers, while others never saw it. If I'd forced the point, it might have led to disaster. I have read novels built up from thematic ideas and found most of them to be a difficult exercise.

A good story produces themes as a byproduct of events. A story focuses on the personal details of character, while the theme reveals the bigger picture. Agatha Christie wrote mystery novels that repeatedly show how crime doesn't pay. Mary Shelley's *Frankenstein* is classic science fiction that demonstrates man's desire to explain God through science. *The Three Little Pigs* is pure drama that says you should never be too big or too proud. I am uncertain if those writers started out to prove those points, but their themes emerged, and the writer brought the point home.

EXERCISES

When story drama seems lacking, employ the scene and sequel method. Select a troublesome scene from your current work and uncover its dramatic core by answering the questions associated with the aforementioned plotting techniques. Focusing in this way allows you to refine and fortify the purpose of a scene. Also, try it on a scene from your favorite writer and analyze the results.

Select a compelling news story from your local paper and identify the dramatic core of events. Whose story is it? What was their goal? What problems did they encounter? Who or what stood in the way? How did it end up? What did they learn? These questions help illuminate the essence of human drama.

VII. Professional Revisions

*"Something made greater by ourselves
and in turn that makes us greater."*
— *Maya Angelou*

All fine writing is the result of rewriting. I don't know who coined that phrase, but it is certainly a fact. The first draft is the art of writing. It should be accomplished as uninhibited as possible, held apart from the unforgiving conscience of the self-editor. The style of draft work varies between authors, from a bare bones outline to pregnant prose. Revising the draft involves the craft of writing. Prose is expanded and contracted, and elucidation is achieved. Writers spend most of their time rewriting. They make up for their perceived deficiencies in talent and level the playing field.

Another important precept of writing is that all drafts are bad. Bad is a general category, ranging from *not too bad* to *pretty damn bad*. In draft work, writers sometimes deliver lines that are pretty damn bad. An honest writer admits that the draft process is an inescapable flirtation with disaster. As he attempts to elevate his prose, he sometimes misses and suffers a bad fall. This is expected. The revision process exists to recognize the fall and mop up the mess, and readers never witness the accident. Readers seek the ease of flawlessness.

THE FIRST LOOK

Revision requires time and space. Allow time to forget the prose and return with the fresh eyes of a reader. After a story is drafted, put it aside and work on something different. This is also true during the revision process. The prose becomes so familiar that the writer anticipates the words before reading them. When I spend too much time with a piece, my eyes see earlier versions, regardless of the words on the paper. I'm reading in my mind, instead of the pages in front of me.

Juxtaposing the cathartic process of draft work with the labor-intensive act of revision creates balance in the day-to-day life of a writer. Take a break during the draft of a story to write a nonfiction piece to completion. While performing lengthy revisions, pause to design your next creative project. One process feeds the other. It is a lot like absorbing and releasing energy.

After giving the draft work a rest, read it through with little or no pause. Prepare to be both surprised and embarrassed with the words on the paper. A writer delivers stunning lines in the draft, gems that pass from revision to revision untouched. A writer also drafts lousy prose – inappropriate, limp, or downright goofy phrases. Both good and ugly writing leap off the page. Keep the good, knock down the ugly, and aspire to elevate the mediocre.

This book introduces the elements of a solid story and methods for obtaining them. Try to embrace a few techniques, while modifying others to suit your storytelling approach. The following section details a process for draft revision. Take what you can use and incorporate it into your own revision process. Make note of the revision aspects that you like the least. Those are probably areas where you need work.

LEVEL ONE: THE OPENING

The opening is the first scene in a story, albeit a very crucial scene. It introduces the main character, her hopes and desires, and the point of view. Those are story basics, and not until they are known does the story get rolling.

The tricky part about drafting an opening is that this is the time when a writer knows the least about the characters and plot. Most writers agree that it takes roughly 100 pages to understand the main characters. This often invalidates earlier characterizations, and as a result, character desire and behavior seem unfocused or incorrect. Some writers toss out the first 100 pages and start over. That is a drastic measure, although it is common to labor over the first fifty pages and definitely the first twenty-five.

When revising, the opening must be arresting before I proceed. Everything falls out of the first line. Some writers say that the first line gives away the ending. Indeed, the opening scene starts the journey, and if it must change, the entire story path might change along with it. Try to get the opening in order before addressing the remaining story. You may return to tweak the prose, but it will be structurally sound before you edit the rest.

Chapter II of this book covers the important elements of story openings. Below is a checklist for review. The first three items are vital to the success of launching a story.

Introduce the Main Character
Show Predominant Point of View
Reveal the Story Question
Preview the Setting
Create Action
Set the Tone
Shorten the Timeline & Create Order

LEVEL TWO: STRUCTURE/CONTENT

With the opening in place, consider the structure and content of the story. Analyze character, setting, plot, and their relationship to one another. Changes at this point may affect the entire story structure, causing new scenes to appear or existing scenes to disappear. Work at a high level to establish the arc of the story. Why perfect the details of a scene if it might be removed from the entire piece?

Verify the Plot

Is there at least one strong dramatization per chapter? Don't let a chapter go by without serious conflict among the characters. Readers anticipate it.

Does every scene serve the story question? Scenes progress the story question, for better or worse, otherwise they wander off the thread of the story. This is the time to add and remove scenes as needed.

Does the conflict heighten en route to the climax? When the drama heightens, that becomes the new plateau for the story arc. It eventually becomes routine, unless the drama escalates. Keep raising the stakes for the characters during the story. The climax is a natural outgrowth of the pressure cooker constructed along the story journey.

Are there too many coincidences? Coincidence is a helpful device for stories. Life forms pleasant occurrences, but if major plot points often hinge on chance encounters, the story becomes unbelievable. Limit it to one or two, although even one coincidence might be more than the story can bear. If a rare moon rock falls out of the sky and into the bed of Joe's pickup truck, while he is on the way to a lunar geologist's convention, where a million dollar prize for the top rock will be awarded, that might be more coincidence than the reader can handle. Keep coincidences subtle and useful.

Is there unneeded repetition? Repetition in grade school was useful, if not overbearing. Repetition in stories is useful to set up a later event. If Jane always parks her car in the same spot and suddenly changes to another, it might demonstrate a character change. In comedy, repetition sets up jokes. If Bob always sinks a hole in one on the golf course, it might be funny to see him miss when we most expect it. Repetition draws attention, and readers notice, but if Jane is always having a bad hair day, it begins to look silly.

Verify Character Details

Do character details appear in the story? Some level of character detail must exist for everyone in the story, even if they are only brief encounters for the reader.

Are the details proportional to importance? Apply character details in relation to their significance in the story. Every word builds a reader's expectations. Secondary characters don't deserve the detail required for primary characters.

Are the details consistent? If Jane has blue eyes or talks with a lisp on page 10, she will also have those attributes on page 200, unless appropriate explanation supports the change.

Are the details different? If every woman has blonde hair and a 38-inch chest, the story better take place inside the Playboy Mansion.

Is the dialogue realistic? Spoken language is casual, casting aside the rigid conventions of the written word. It is situational, attempting to address the line previously spoken. A single line of dialogue is a component of the whole conversation and often indecipherable when standing alone. If characters are sketched with uniqueness and clarity, they will speak for themselves, defining the parameters of their language, moods, and attitudes.

> "I've got the stuff," Bob said.
> "The what?" Jane replied.
> "You know, the stuff."
> "I hate that garbage."
> "You always hate it."
> "There you go again."
> "Don't start."
> "I'm not the one starting."

Is there too much dialect? Some writers seek authenticity by recording dialogue verbatim, especially with the use of slang and accents. This is cumbersome to read. Pepper the dialogue with dialect, and readers will get the point, mentally filling in the blanks. It is better to know what a character is trying to say, than replicating speech with exactness.

Verify Setting Details

Do setting details appear in the story? Some level of setting detail must exist for each scene, even if we are only passing through a room. Otherwise the story is subject to 'white room' syndrome, where characters move in time and space with no sense of their surroundings.

Are the details proportional to importance? Apply setting details in relation to their significance in the story. Every word builds a reader's expectations. If the writer spends a lot of time describing a certain aspect of setting, readers believe it to be vital to the story.

Are the details consistent? If Jane's car is red on page 10, she will have a red car on page 200, unless appropriate explanation supports the change.

Are the details different? Variety in all aspects of the story entices mental acuity for the reader. In other words, it keeps people from becoming bored.

Are the details correct? This is the time to verify factual information. Correct assumptions about location and lifestyle (i.e. geography, professions, language, etc). These aspects illuminate the prose, yet invalidate a story if they are incorrect.

LEVEL THREE: STYLE

When the storyline is set and the character and setting details are brought into focus, concentrate on prose. A writer's style of storytelling is evident from the beginning of the tale's construction. It is an extension of his brain and the way he absorbs and interprets the world around him. With the arc of the story set, it is time to clarify the prose, as only he can do it.

Establish Consistent Tone

Tone refers to the quality and pitch of the prose. It is the emotional resonance of the story, albeit humorous, horrifying, or dramatic. Whatever the tone, search for inconsistent passages that sabotage the integrity of the story.

Simplify Sentence Structure

Always look to prune and clarify sentences. Be concise. One powerful phrase might replace a few fuzzier statements. At times, writers struggle for an exact description, circling the point with a collection of words. Take a moment to uncover the precise description in one brief phrase.

Vary Sentence Structure

The length and construction of sentences serve different purposes. Action scenes require crisp short sentences to maintain the pace. Long sentences serve panoramic scenes or deep introspection. Poetic phrases work for romance and comedy. See what works for your scenes. Play with the sentence structure.

Vary Paragraph, Scene, and Chapter Length

Changes keep readers attentive. Blocks of paragraphs of equal length create a visual monotony. I am getting sleepy just thinking about it. The same goes for scene and chapter lengths. Try a scene that is only one paragraph long or a chapter of just two pages. Search for variety.

Examine Word Choice

Root out vagueness. Replace words like *something, anything,* and *everything* with concrete nouns.

The *thing* about dessert is the calories.
The *problem* with dessert is the calories.

Select strong verbs. Replace verbs like *was, is, would, should,* and *could* with powerful and engaging verbs.

He *was* at the top of the corporate ladder, but he *would* rather be home with his family.
He *fought* his way to the top of the corporate ladder, but he *missed* his family at home.

Too many adjectives? Change noun and adjective combinations into one strong noun.

Tom drove the *thin nail* into the *orange-yellow* skin of the fruit.
Tom drove the *brad* into the *ocher* skin of the fruit.

Too many adverbs? Change verb and adverb combinations into one strong verb.

She *slowly walked* into the boardroom.
She *sauntered* into the boardroom.

Reduce compound descriptions. Use discrete words that relay the point. Observe the following passage:

A small, deep purple 3x5 note arrived in the mail. Joe recognized his former wife's handwriting. She wanted him to return their children. She was coming to visit in a few days.

The passage might sound better as:

Joe's ex-wife dropped him a maroon postcard: 'I want the kids back. See you soon.'

Find the right word. Employ a thesaurus and dictionary. The appropriate word is out there for the taking.

Remove 'said' and 'thought'

The person thinking or speaking in a story is often implied by his position in the text. Be creative. Use action or narration alongside the thought or dialogue to identify its owner. In the following example, use of the words 'said' and 'thought' are unnecessary to identify Jane as the person doing the speaking and thinking.

> Jane took the horse by the reins. "Git!" She dug in her spurs. *I hope this old mare's got enough left to make it.*

Remove Instances of "Fine Writing"

Track down instances of fine writing and remove them. Fine writing occurs during wonderfully unnatural stretches of prose. It might be the flowery description of the chipped table in the office or the overblown insight to the human condition. When the writer pens these lines at 3 A.M., they often appear brilliant, but when they hit daylight, they are exposed like a pink bowtie. They are funny and overdone, when they intend otherwise. Readers will roll their eyes because the writer is trying too hard to impress.

Read Aloud

Reading the prose aloud identifies errant and clumsy passages. The writer stumbles over poor words, phrases, and sentences. Unnatural dialogue hits the ear like a spitball. Read your work aloud within the safe confines of your working space before exposing your errors to the public.

LEVEL FOUR: PRESENTATION

With the hardest work in place, take time to examine the basics of language, before submitting your work to agents and editors. Mistakes in this category should never occur, but too often I receive student prose with grammar and spelling errors. Solid presentation separates you as a professional writer in every form of the medium, from advertising copy to fine literature. Make a habit of presenting clean copy.

Basic Order

Put stimulus and response in the proper order. The following is out of order.

Joe hit the ground, hearing the explosion.

Organize phrases and sentences in order of occurrence. The following sentence is out of order.

Joe won the race, after he filled out the entry application.

Build lists in order of increasing importance or impact. Without intending to be outrageous, the following is out of order.

Joe had a pretty bad year. His dog died. His wife left him. His computer caught fire. His mail arrived at the wrong address, and he stubbed a toe.

The passage suggests that Joe's priorities are clearly

out of whack. If this isn't the case, the story must present a reasonable justification for Joe's thinking.

Grammar

Obtain *The Elements of Style* by Strunk and White, and memorize the first eleven rules. The English language is sinking into a lexicon of paraphrases, slang, buzzwords, and acronyms. Soon you will be one of the few remaining people who can still write and speak the language.

Spelling

Most of us work on a computer with a word processor. It is easy to check spelling. Don't get caught with spelling errors, or you will appear as if you didn't care enough to proofread your words. When in doubt, consult a dictionary. Computers won't catch 'bear' when you meant to use 'bare.'

EXECUTING REVISIONS

The four level revision process in this book is a top down approach. Work the levels in iterations. Be comfortable with the work at one level, before moving onto the next. This builds the structure of the story before fixing the mess wrought by the construction. It also saves time. Why perfect a scene or paragraph that might not remain in the finished version? Upon passing from level two to three, a solid story stands in place. All scenes will remain on the storyline and in their current position. It is now a matter of making them resonate in the reader's mind.

A story is a unique creation, requiring a special effort to complete. During the draft process, pause to make note of ideas, weaknesses, and potential areas of research. I record story ideas and research information in a composition book. I also number revision concerns from the last page toward the front. I fill six to ten pages of notes on grammar, theme, tone, research requirements, and other specific story concerns. These are concrete problems, and I won't slow the momentum of the draft to solve them. I might use too many passive verbs or fudge the details of an unfamiliar profession. Bad habits and the assumption of guesswork as fact are two comfortably dangerous behaviors, but the back of my composition book saves me, detailing my story's shortcomings. It holds a checklist of needed revisions.

While good draft work is often brave and ground-breaking, the revision process requires another kind of courage. It is akin to self-surgery, knowing when to amputate one of your limbs. Be ruthless with your prose. If a word, sentence, scene, or chapter doesn't serve the story, lop it off. It might contain the most brilliant prose of the piece, but it is cancer to the story, driving it off course and killing reader interest. Save it for another day. It might form the centerpiece of a new story. Trust your ability to think of even better words down the line.

SOLICITING FEEDBACK

There comes a point when a writer desires objectivity. Cultivate a trusted reader. I have a target reader in mind when

I write, someone who appreciates the same aspects of story-telling. She knows when I miss the mark, and she is not afraid to tell me. I argue. I curse and moan, but in the end, I know she is right. She is not a writer. She is a reader. She doesn't stay up at night considering character flaws or lifestyle elements. She knows a good story. She laughs. She cries. She is entertained, and if I cannot do this for her, I have missed my objective.

Beyond that, build a reading circle. This is also composed of readers. Writers are a dangerous group to critique a work in progress. Each writer has a personal vision of a story, and it is often not yours. Good members of a reading circle are well read. They are just as happy with a biography of FDR, as the latest Robert Stone. They pick up *TV Guide* and *The Economist* in the same shopping trip. They love the written word. They are authorities to give the thumbs up or down on your work. They are a mere sample of the reading public. Try to remove your emotion and listen to them.

WHEN IS A STORY FINISHED?

Who knows? There comes a time when a writer must put the work down and move on. Writers often get a brainstorm and return to a particular piece with ideas to elevate the story, but overall, a point arrives when the writer can go no further and must let it rest on its laurels.

For my first published novel, I accepted countless pieces of advice from editors and agents, tweaking each nuance of the story. I reached a point where I was changing sentences because I was tired of reading the same lines over and over. I'd clearly spent too long with the story. I finally threw my hands up and told my writing mentor that I was finished accepting the often inane feedback leveled on my novel. An amazing thing happened. It was a moment out of a grainy kung fu movie. "Son," my mentor said. "You're ready to go to the next level."

When the work is as good as it can be, move on. Begin another story. Hope for enlightenment, but learn when to quit spinning your wheels. If Michelangelo sought perfection – and he was darn near perfect in his art – he'd have chipped away at the statue of David, until it was small enough to clip on a key chain.

Finally, be patient with your talent at its current level. If you aspire to improve, you will sacrifice and work every day. You will get better. You will tell the stories you want to tell. Great artists learn to work in a vacuum, producing ideal works of art that hold a mirror to humanity, society, and themselves. Be brave.

EXERCISES

Outline your revision process. What do your talents require? Are you concentrating on your weaknesses? Can the ordinary be elevated?

Resurrect your old writing and run it through the aforementioned revision process. If the work is old enough, certain flaws will immediately stand out. See if the process doesn't improve the story structure and prose.

VIII. The View Toward Manhattan

*"I think that New York is not the cultural
center of America, but the business and
administrative center of American culture."*
— *Saul Bellow*

Along the path to publishing, writers collect untold
numbers of rejections. My path was no different. I was not a
literary insider. I earned no degrees in fine arts, journalism, or
literature and never labored inside a publishing house, yet I
gained valuable experience and success in each of those areas.
I waded through countless rejections and sought the help of a
trusted mentor. I concentrated on the craft and art of storytelling and learned to trust my instincts.

An aspiring writer should cast off discouragement.
Regardless of the endeavor, the path to success is riddled with
uninspired individuals who will say "no, no, and no." Eventually someone will say "yes" or lend a helping hand. In the
process of enlightenment, you might just answer that second
ancient question: Why am I here?

A GLIMPSE INSIDE THE IVORY TOWER

To many writers, the Manhattan publishing world looks like a series of impenetrable, remote ivory towers full of people who select new work indiscriminately. I understand that impression. I held it for almost decade. I will try to make sense of it.

The organizational structure of a publishing house is the closest I have witnessed to academia. The hierarchy is linear. Departments and imprints exist on a straight line, barely answering to a central authority. The corporate mergers of the 80's and 90's have muddled the view and complicated the duplication of services. Advances in technology forced rapid changes on the industry. Departments, imprints, and whole publishing houses crumbled. But the people involved in the day-to-day operations of publishing are men and women who love books. They work long hours and read piles of manuscripts. They adore the written word, but no matter what any of them believe about the higher art of literature, a publishing house exists to sell books and make money.

Publishing is primarily a business, and the bulk of it exists in Manhattan. Reread the quote at the head of this chapter. Saul Bellow was right on the money. Don't think a publishing house will do anything that you cannot do for yourself. They will not fix bad grammar, chubby plots, and stilted characters. An author needs to deliver a watertight story and get it to the right people. The rest is fate and luck, and as successful businessmen say, we create our own luck. A solid story creates a lot of luck for a writer.

From an industry perspective, a good book is a book that sells. The research behind this comes from years of experience. If you read the publishing trade journals or spend an afternoon in a bookstore, you'll observe the following. The cover of the book entices a reader to pull it from the shelf. The first page and author photo sell the book. Talk to anyone in the business, and they know this. It is the contents of the book that sells the author's next book. We have all been duped by a snazzy new writer – the next great literary child genius perhaps – only to find that the story goes nowhere. On the other hand, we have discovered great new writers this way.

To a lesser extent, potential book buyers flip through the pages to gauge the amount of dialogue. Modern readers love dialogue. It is the most engaging and voyeuristic element of storytelling. We can blame television, film, or even theater for this preference and stick with endless narrative in our prose. We can also run headlong into a 100 mile per hour wind. We are likely to be more successful exploiting dialogue in our stories.

Publishing people mimic the reading habits of common readers. "How's that?" you say. "They should know better." They do know better. They understand what readers want. If you ask me, they understand it a little too well. Right now, editors and agents are culling through our submissions, anticipating reader reaction. They are searching for the most compelling manuscripts, but they must work within the needs of the business. It pays their salaries and finances the office coffeemaker. A book must sell, and a book is sold when a reader decides to take it home.

THE EDITORIAL PIZZA PARTY

Like any business, employees desire to ascend the corporate ladder. Junior editors want to be senior editors, and senior editors want their own imprints or a nameplate that reads 'Editor-in-Chief.' They stake their careers on the success of the manuscripts that they bring forward. That might be your manuscript, polished and ready for review.

I have heard the following story so many times from people in the industry that it must be true. It has been referred to as the manuscript shooting gallery and housecleaning day. I've also heard this called, 'the editorial pizza party.'

Picture several eager junior editors surrounding a conference table in the early evening. The big guns have gone home, and the junior editors are tired, hungry, and overworked. Someone orders enough pizza and sodas to fill their stomachs, as they eliminate the latest crop of unknown authors from the running.

In front of each editor stands a stack of potential manuscripts. This is a small percentage of the original submissions. Many have been eliminated because the work simply did not fit the publisher's needs. Others get rejected due to lousy query letters or poor manuscript presentation. On the other hand, some manuscripts gain the inside track: a top agent calls, an author carries respectable credentials, or even better, a writer proves herself in smaller markets. The manuscripts at this stage carry a certain level of expectation. An editor believes that this is both what the publisher needs and what the public desires from a book.

At the editorial pizza party, Associate Editor Jane swipes the first manuscript off the stack. It is by you, an unpublished author. Great, you have made it this far. You've no doubt written a compelling query letter and connected with the right people.

Jane reads the title. "April in Paris." She searches the faces of her associates for interest. Most recognize your play on the classic jazz title, except for Bob who spills diet cola on his beige khakis again, but we will ignore him.

Overall, their interest is good for your manuscript. If you don't seize their attention with the title, much like a reader standing before the new release rack in the book store, the manuscript is history, stuffed into your self-addressed stamped envelop or dumped into the paper recycler. At this point, you've earned a terse letter from the publisher, which rarely explains the rejection in a meaningful way.

Next, Jane reads the first line, and a couple of editors raise their eyes. Your prose is stunning.

She finishes the paragraph. They like what they hear. Even Bob is listening. Your story holds their attention.

It is not an accident that most opening paragraphs touch on many story elements at once. Accomplished writers fight to be noticed from the first sentence.

Picture a story opening as a series of hurdles: title, first line, first paragraph, first page, and first scene of approximately five to ten pages. If it stumbles over one hurdle, it is out of the race. If it clears them all, the manuscript garners further consideration. It will probably still be rejected, but this time with a nice handwritten note. That is further than most, and hold onto that note. You have just developed an industry contact – someone interested in your type of work.

THE TITLE IS READ FIRST

Authors don't have much control over the cover of their novel, nor should they, unless they are graphic artists. Publishing houses employ skilled artists who understand visual presentation and proper color selection. They know that men and women select different designs and colors from the shelf. It is a science, studied for years by talented marketers.

On the other hand, a novel's title is under the writer's control. A title should be outstanding; an invitation to read that beckons louder than the others. Of course it must also relate to the story. Take a moment and browse the bookstore shelves. See what titles capture your attention. Chances are these titles are succinct and meaningful. Some are horrifying or shocking. Some pose a question. Most are positive in one sense or another. Others are funny or absurd, a play on common phases or stereotypes. Some capture everything in a single word.

Titles are not copyrighted. We may reuse famous titles verbatim. This evokes the mood and emotion of the previous work. If that effect is desired, try a variation of a well-known title. This works particularly well for comic effect, such as *Fast Times on Cannery Row*, *The Scarlet Postcard*, or *The Invisible Dog*.

Titles are advertisements for the written work. I had worried about the title of *Jesus Lives in Trenton*. It managed to rile both the left and right wing factions. The right found it blasphemous, even though the story is not, and the left feared it might be a religious book, which it isn't either. My publisher understood that a strong public reaction is a positive asset. Both good and bad responses sell books. It is the banal stuff in the middle that doesn't help.

Don't fret over stark reactions to your title or work. Here are a veteran rock star's comments on the topic of negative criticism: "For one thing, it goes with the territory, period. For another, they are talking about you, and this sometimes works in your favor because many people cannot read and comprehend written text, and it is only important that your name appeared in print, conversation, or whatever."

When designing a title, be brave. When writing, be fearless. Don't save ideas for later. Use them now. You will think of better ideas down the line to take their place. If you have an exciting title or story idea that upsets common thought, ignore unenlightened responses. The worst that might happen is the story will get noticed. Your most ardent detractors will unwittingly join your promotional team, and your story will become an overnight success.

EXERCISES

Go to the bookstore and browse the new releases. See what titles attract your attention. Analyze why they work for you.

Later, get a private vantage point where you can watch the same bookshelf. Observe how potential readers browse the selections. Notice the titles they remove from the shelf. Watch how they examine the cover and thumb through the pages. These are editors looking at your work, the purest and least prejudiced editors of them all. If you don't learn anything about books, you will have fun watching people. Notice their clothes, hair, mumblings, and stirrings. We are each strange in our own way.

IX. Connecting with the Industry

"Something there that doesn't love a wall,
And wants it down."
— Robert Frost

The publishing industry is waiting for new work, and although the business seems impenetrable and unyielding, new authors are accepted on a regular basis. This is a professional industry where a writer's words are reprinted and distributed to the public in a variety of mediums. Rules of decorum exist. Professionalism and courtesy are valued before the prose gets a first glance.

Every business has standard methods of communication. A writer develops four basic tools for contacting the publishing industry, and throughout the writer's career, this varies little. These are the query letter, synopsis, manuscript, and most overlooked, the writer of the work.

QUERY LETTER

For most writers, the query letter is their initial missive to the industry. Craft the most concise, direct, and clean letter possible. Give the agent or editor a reason to look at the prose. If the writer cannot compose a brief, cogent, and error free letter, serious doubt arises about the prose to follow. Like the manuscript, there are no excuses for grammatical errors, discussing unrelated topics, or saying too much. Multi-page queries are death to the unknown writer. If some editors or agents see a query run off the page, they cast it aside. A lousy query assures rejection.

Here are the vital components of a query letter:

The Contact: Address the letter to a living and breathing person. Avoid the 'Dear Editor' or 'Dear Agent' salutation. These letters are addressed to no one, and it is likely that no one will read them.

Prior Relationship: If you are contacting someone for a special reason, mention that in the first line of the letter. Maybe you read about that agent in the news, a similar or favorite book was edited by this person, or a published author gave a referral. This is an appropriate time to include names and circumstances, and if you have contacted this publishing entity on a prior occasion, remind them of the positive aspects of your last encounter.

Introduction: In one or two sentences, state who you are and your important writing credentials. If you don't have credentials, don't invent them, and don't mention your stint editing the high school newsletter either.

Work for Sale: Mention the title of the work for sale and a brief description. It should be evident why this is so important. Only the title and a brief description of the story or article appear in a query. Like a book on a shelf, the title catches the reader's fancy, while the jacket blurb entices them to read. These are the hooks for your work. For an unknown or unpublished writer, this is the most important part of the query letter. Place it as close as possible to the beginning.

Relevant Credentials: State why you are qualified to write this piece. If you are connected with a leading authority on the topic, mention that up front in the letter.

Tie-ins: Is there a current events topic or common school of thought to which this piece relates? From the first day of acceptance, the marketing department will ponder ways to generate publicity. Relationships to popular topics are a godsend. Certain topics sell themselves. There will always be cookbooks, diet books, and books by celebrities.

Expectations: Depending on the publishing entity, state whether you desire representation for your work or the actual sale of your work.

Material Response: Publishing entities appreciate disposable manuscripts. Paper is cheap, while postage is increasingly expensive, especially for book length material. Paper can be recycled, but it takes time and effort to stuff a manuscript in a bag and carry it around. Always include a self-addressed stamped envelope (SASE) of standard business letter size for the publishing entity to respond.

The appendix includes actual query letters for both a short story and novel. Both of these letters led to positive relationships. They are sales pitches for my work. I deliver my relevant accomplishments up front and state what is for sale and why the publisher might desire it. I spawn interest for the agent or editor to at least glance at my prose.

SYNOPSIS

The synopsis is a summary of the story, novel, or article for sale. It comes in various lengths, and while seeking publication, the shorter versions rest on the tip of your tongue. Prepare them in advance of possible interest.

One Sentence Synopsis: It is possible to summarize any story, article, or book in one intriguing sentence. Publishing houses do it every day. As you travel the planet, you will encounter helpful people or at least people who know people in the publishing industry. You never know when you will be stuck in an elevator with the wife of a senior editor. I know this from personal experience. Be ready to pitch your work at all times, and the one sentence summary does the trick. Anyone can carry a brief and cogent sentence to the right people. In the appendix examples, you will find a one-sentence summary up front in each of the query letters.

Short Paragraph Synopsis: This is a paragraph length description of your work. It is used in query letters and on anyone willing to listen. It will run three to five sentences.

One Page Synopsis: The one page summary is often requested by editors and agents in addition to the manuscript or sample pages.

Full Synopsis: This is the true chapter-by-chapter summary of your work. Lengths vary from four to twenty-five pages. It is not a blow-by-blow recitation, but an encapsulation of characters and dramatic events. It covers the highlights and sequences. It reveals the dramatic arc of a story.

The one page or full synopsis is often included with submissions to editors and agents. Seek their individual submission guidelines in one of the readily available guides to the industry. The appendix contains an example synopsis for the novel, *Jesus Lives in Trenton*.

MANUSCRIPT

When the happy day arrives that a publishing entity requests your manuscript, put it in the best possible shape. Some of the suggestions below sound picky, but try reading the volume of work that passes through the hands of an editor or agent. Anything that resembles an annoyance needs to be removed. You want your prose to stand out, not your lousy manuscript presentation.

Is the manuscript complete? Fiction must be complete. Nonfiction can be sold with an outline and sample chapters.

Is the work solid? Has the work gone through enough revision cycles? If doubt exists, give it one more pass. Try reading it through, examining passages where you pause.

Don't get fancy. Avoid pictures, unless absolutely vital to the piece. Skip italics, bold, and fancy script. The prose should imply shifts in narrative or tone without special effects. In *All the Pretty Horses*, Cormac McCarthy writes dialogue without use of quotation marks, but we still sense when the characters are speaking apart from the narrative.

Use clean white paper. I recommend at least 20lb paper; otherwise the ink from the next page becomes visible while reading the top of the stack.

Double-spaced pages are required. The space for two horizontal lines of text is used for one. It is easier to make notes, as well as gentler on the eyes.

Left-justify the text. Words are evenly spaced to the left margin. The unevenly spaced words of centered text rapidly becomes tiresome to the eyes.

Use standard margins. Page margins are at least one inch surrounding the text.

Create chapter heads. Chapters, as well as the start of a short story, begin one third of the way down the page. The short story or chapter title is first, followed by a standard break of three blank lines before the body of the text. It is a good idea to number chapters, even if the numbers don't appear in the final printing.

Place identifying details on each page. Excluding the title page, the upper left corner of every page shows your name, a running page count, and the title. A shortened version of the title is fine. Pages are numbered from the first page to the last, without exception, although the title page for a novel is not included in the page count.

Include the title page. Novel and short story manuscripts have different title pages. A novel has a separate page, while a short story includes author details on the first page of the prose.

Remember the end. At the end of the piece, type the words 'The End.' in the center, after three blank lines.

The appendix shows the manuscript format for both a novel and short story, including sample title pages.

THE WRITER

The writer as a person is perhaps the most overlooked aspect of marketing new work. By nature, a writer prefers to hide in a cave and produce written words, but when a book is published, the author attracts potential readers before the prose is examined. While there are exceptions to this behavior, authors must emerge from their hovels and greet the world. Recall the processes of selling a book. The title draws it off the shelf, and the first page and author photo sell the book.

Beneath the author photo is a brief biography. It is the core of what readers find interesting about the author. Writers would do well by shaping that persona from the very beginning. I haven't worked in the space program for a decade, but it is what first attracts readers to my work: the former space physicist, turned stay-at-home dad, turned author and teacher.

In your query letters and correspondences with the industry, search for ways to marry yourself to your work. The publishing industry desires authors, as well as good stories. Let people know who you are. Stories are often natural outgrowths of personal experiences, and one or more may be exploited to your advantage. In truth, the author is marketed alongside the book.

WHAT IS AN AGENT?

There are hundreds of literary agents, but there are less good agents. Good agents believe in their authors, and they sell work similar to that author's work. They are in close contact with the publishing industry and understand the corporate landscape. They make friends in publishing houses. They take editors to lunch and make phone calls. Essentially, literary agents are salespeople. Good salespeople have good contacts. They are people persons. They know how to intrigue potential buyers. They can turn negatives into positives and make everyone feel satisfied. It is a skill that many writers lack. This is why a writer hires an agent. They work for the writer, and the fee ranges from ten to twenty percent of the writer's literary income.

A great agent is well worth the price. They seek the largest possible advance for your work. An advance is the projected royalties, paid by the publisher in advance, to the author. The size of the advance affirms the publisher's belief in a book's potential sales. A large advance is a self-fulfilling prophecy. The publisher will work hard to recover a large initial cash outlay. It makes sense.

Generally speaking, top agents don't want to hear from unproven writers. Why? They are the best in the business. They already handle successful people. They take on clients from referrals and cherry pick the up and coming new authors. When my first novel hit a second printing, good agents took serious notice of my work. Before then, I had agents that did nothing that I couldn't have done for myself. They mailed letters to people that they didn't really know and collected rejection slips. I published my first novel without an agent.

Beginning writers want to find an agent, but it is the work that sells. Their writing must be in the best shape to attract a decent agent, and if the writer concentrates on the elements of storytelling, she allows a chance for her finest work to emerge. That is what writers do. They deliver their best prose to the public and watch what happens. Behind great prose is a solid story. When some agents spot a new talent in one of the top magazines or with a small press, they are tempted to contact that writer.

LOCATING AGENTS & EDITORS

When locating an agent or editor, look for people who represent work similar to yours. People who sell and publish children's books know mostly people in that genre. The same is true for every category. If an agent sells murder mysteries, she knows the people who buy them. The guides to the literary markets and agencies list the titles bought and sold by various entities in the business. Create a target list for your work.

Another way to narrow the possibilities is by performing a reverse search. Investigate books similar to yours. On the spine or inside the cover is the publisher and possibly the editor and agent who bought and sold the book. Pick up the phone and call the publisher to seek the editor of the book. In many cases, the editor will tell you the name of the agent who sold the book, and while you have the editor on the phone, it is the perfect opportunity to sell your book. Recall the one sentence and one paragraph story synopsis that resides on the tip of your tongue. It's show time. Here is an editor who has purchased a book similar to yours. Make a pitch for your work.

Don't forget networking. Mentioning someone or something familiar to that agent or editor will promote a fair look at your work. In a crowded field, that is your objective.

Finally, if an agent becomes interested in your work, interview her. She will be working for you, and in the end, you will forgo a large chunk of your income for her services. Ask her who she knows and where your book fits into the scheme of things. If you don't receive acceptable answers, consider your options.

SUBMISSION ETIQUETTE

With a list of potential editors and agents, work within the acceptable rules. Most publishing entities have guidelines. These are listed in the widely available guides to the market or received directly from the publishing entities. They state the type of work accepted, the format of submitted materials, the writers who qualify for submission, and how long they take to respond. Most entities accept specific categories of work. Not all accept unpublished authors or unsolicited requests. Some want just a query letter first. Others want sample chapters and a synopsis, and some want the entire book. Their guidelines spell out specific requirements, and ignoring them shows that you didn't bother or don't care. Both behaviors display a lack of professionalism and waste everyone's time, including your postage and paper. Let your time amount to more than dead trees.

Multiple submissions are taboo in the industry, especially if the guidelines clearly state so. A multiple submission means that two or more people are looking at the manuscript at the same time. Off the record, many agents say, "do it, but be reasonable." It is ludicrous for a publishing entity to make a writer wait three months to a year for a response to sample chapters. Life is only so long. A writer might die waiting for a rejection slip, but draw the line at the entire manuscript. No more than one entity may review the entire manuscript at any given time. It is a commitment to read an entire work, and if someone requests it, assume they have serious interest.

When submitting work, form a plan. Query five to ten people at once, wait a month, and query more. The query list should be well honed from the writer's industry research. If more than one agent responds positively, send the requested materials, but again draw the line at the entire manuscript.

After the work is submitted, don't become a pest. Don't fax, call, or e-mail. That will earmark you as an impatient and unreasonable individual. The publishing industry moves like a machine, each gear clicking into place at its appointed time. A writer can do very little to expedite the process. After ninety days, send a note inquiring about the work. If the response is unacceptable, determine to press on with others, even if they hold the entire manuscript.

Keep track of responses. If someone cannot respond to your work within three months, it is likely they will never respond in a favorable fashion. Most people have difficult and busy times in their lives but not every day and all year long. Keep note of who handled work poorly, and avoid them in the future. Remember who responded quickly and professionally. Put a star next to those who inked a personal note. This is a golden response. Agents and editors are very busy, yet some aspect of the work made them take notice. Even if the work was rejected, put this name aside. This is a contact. Send this person revisions or new work. After a while, most writers develop a small pool of contacts.

Above all, remember that this is the publishing industry. It is populated by individuals who love books in all shapes and sizes. They cannot inject talent into a soulless writer, and they haven't the time to build the craft of an undisciplined writer, although they hunt daily for someone who gives them pause. The discovery of a talented new writer makes everyone's day and perhaps a publishing individual's career, including the new author's career. Learn your craft, polish your work, and place yourself in position to be that author.

BREAKING INTO THE BUSINESS

If you are tired of publishers returning your brilliant stories faster than you can lick the stamp for an SASE, start freelancing. Nothing builds your confidence and credentials faster than getting your name in print.

For a variety of financial reasons, newspapers and magazines offer immediate opportunities. From your local farm report to *The New York Times*, reporting staffs have been trimmed, and freelancers provide much of their output. You can even pitch an article or feature story over the Internet. (Look for freelance opportunities at www.WritersNotes.com.)

Freelancing often pays little, yet many writers sustain a decent income through resale rights. You will learn how to compose concise and intelligent prose under a deadline. These are important skills for a professional writer. You will also be networking in the business, and it almost always leads to your next opportunity. On the other hand, filing publisher's rejection slips doesn't offer many rewards beyond basic secretarial skills and the chance to one day go on anti-depressants.

EXERCISES

Construct the one and two sentence synopsis for your articles and stories, and try them out on people. See if they relate the essence of your ideas.

Begin crafting query letters for your projects. Like revising manuscripts, spend time away from the letters and return to update them. You'll discover areas to improve, trimming the prose and creating further intrigue.

X. Seeking Creativity

Art mimics life, not the other way around. The best artists articulate common thought, reaching many people at once. Artists bring clarity to social undercurrents and universal understanding. They appear to anticipate truth. The notion of life imitating art is the self-important artist rearing his needy little head. Artists document events, through an endless variety of mediums. We capture, dissect, disassemble, reorganize, or reclassify life, but we don't invent it. Humanity is much too random and dangerous to let that happen.

Writers are prisms of life. A prism accepts the presence of light and separates it into all of its visible components. It doesn't invent rainbows, although it exposes a myriad of questions within the spectrum of light. Good writing poses many questions.

In my office is a picture of Albert Einstein, not because he was a great physicist but because he was a great thinker. His mind ran overtime, asking question after question. He believed that he would be finished as a thinker when he couldn't formulate the next question. Luckily that never happened. His notebooks brim with questions and theories that scientists continue to investigate to this day.

Like Einstein, who lived to form the next question, writers seek the questions revealed through the written word. These questions belong to all of us. They present us with an opportunity to change.

SEARCHING FOR STORY IDEAS

Writers encounter good story ideas every minute. Radio, television, and print media burgeon with the seeds of inspiration. From quick news stories to deep biographies, ideas for character, setting, and plot emerge in large and small pieces. Beyond that, your acquaintances, their acquaintances, and even you are fertile ground to till. Look for the winners and losers in life. Hunt for interesting details and intriguing circumstances. Learn to interpret life without judging it.

Break Down Ideas

Notice what attracts you to a particular idea. You are a potential reader, as well as a writer. Analyze the story elements. What was the story question? What was the drama? Who was involved? What were their strengths and weaknesses? What happened? Why did things turn out like they did? Was the setting unique or interesting?

Start twisting the facts. What might be a better story

question? What might be even more dramatic? Who otherwise might be involved? What might be their strengths and weaknesses? What might happen and why? Where might the setting be more interesting?

It is a rarity when a complete idea falls directly from one source, but the culmination of parts or the notion set forth by a circumstance may be enough to spawn a gripping tale. Break down real life examples for the essence of story and use that drama, character, or setting in a work of your own.

Create a Record

Keep track of everything. A writer carries a pen. Jot down notes. Tear out news articles. Get a photocopy. Keep paper beside the bed and in your glove box or briefcase. I don't recommend writing while driving, but a quick note scribbled at the roadside or a stoplight never hurt anyone. Just a word or two will be enough to summon the original thought later, and be certain to record pertinent ideas in the middle of the night. Otherwise the only thing you will recall in the morning is that you have forgotten something important.

Get Organized

Gather every written note into a central area. Keep a composition book for topics, ideas, and bits of prose. Record the date and possible source of information. Entire novel concepts might be spawned in this book, but if you begin a novel, breakout a separate composition book, just for that project.

File news clippings, articles, brochures, photocopies, etc. in the same fashion as the notebooks – one for ideas, separate files for each major project. You may never use a particular piece of information, but if it becomes evident down the road, you will know where to find it.

By adopting a useful organizational system, you will expedite research and eliminate the dread of losing your best ideas. A brainstorm is only useful if you record its details.

WRITER'S BLOCK

I don't have time for writer's block. Whenever I am stuck, I glance at my picture of Einstein and ask: what is the question? I might be searching for answers, but I really need questions. I dive into my character sketches, research materials, and plotting methods. I search for questions, and soon I have them and a whole lot more.

Never sit before a blank page and thrash for words. As you prepare to draft a scene, review a basic series of questions. Where is this going to take place? What time is it? Who is there? What do they want? How will they try to get it? What is at stake for each person? How will events transpire for them? Is this dramatic enough to warrant a scene in the story? Massage the questions. It might spawn more questions, but according to Einstein, that is never a problem. Are you going to argue with Einstein? Good luck.

EXPANDING CREATIVITY

Nothing accelerates the writing process better than regular practice. This is true of any art form. A writer devotes his best hours to writing every day. He makes it his daily ritual. It cannot be stopped. It must be done.

Meditation offers an opportunity to quiet the mind and focus on the moment of inspiration. Be still, and allow unrelated thoughts to rise and fall. The mind is a vast landscape with infinite permutations to track down and discover.

Repetitive motion is another form of meditation. As the body cycles over the familiar mechanics of jogging, walking, and even doing the dishes. The brain wanders into alternative thinking. I once sorted, stacked, and stapled paperwork for an entire school, while considering the outline of a novel. I can do the same with a pile of laundry.

Sleep meditation is an excellent way to expand your work. Go to sleep each night, reviewing the progress of your writing project, up until the point where you last stopped. Do this in cycles, considering drama and other key elements of the scenes or chapters. Hunt for flaws, and in the morning, you'll often have solutions to problems that seemed insurmountable. This method of R.E.M. meditation works well for any problem, but if you are going to spend time sleeping instead of writing, assign a writing task to your brain.

Music inspires moods and creativity. The type of music played evokes emotion in the writer, based on tone and personal experience. Avoid music with lyrics. You don't need someone else's words in your head while trying to compose your own, but if a particular scene includes a musical background, consider playing it during the draft.

WRITE WHAT YOU KNOW

What uninspired genius devised this rule? It wasn't a writer of fiction. If authors heeded those words, the balance of modern literature might encompass little more than travel logs, odes to typewriters and keyboards, and tours of every gin mill in the country. Let's face it. We don't do much else. Tom Clancy was an insurance salesman. That would make a gripping action-packed thriller! Broker Bob Jones is hot on the trail of client Donna Smith. Can he get her to sign a life insurance policy before the monthly quota statements?

Consider the authors of great novels. Was Tom Clancy a Russian submarine commander? Was Thomas Harris a genius cannibal? Was Ralph Ellison an invisible man? I don't think so, but they did the research and wrote from those viewpoints with confidence and style. It is better to say 'know what you write.' That makes more sense. When it comes to choosing your story details, you are only limited by research and the depth of your determination to uncover the details. What interests you? Go after it.

How do you research being an invisible man? Observe anyone handing out flyers on a street corner or in an airport.

FIND YOUR VOICE

On the first night of writing class, I instruct students to write from a single sentence that I provide. I offer little instruction, and there are no right answers. As we read the short bits in the roundtable, people hear the various temperaments of those present. They range from fearless to rigid, from heart-strung to hilarious, from morose to comatose. Everyone

but I associate that state of mind with few other activities in my life.

The process of creating a story is in large part an attempt to prove the validity of your inspiration and ensuing thought. Reach for universal connections to character and reflections of humanity. The story serves as a proof of your basic idea.

When a story comes to fruition, I have sapped it of energy. In a sense, I have devoured it, and in completion, I generally have no desire to revisit the associated characters and subject matter. When I am inevitably asked questions about a story that I create, I look back upon the landscape and characters involved like people that I knew in the past. They were real to me once, and now both they and I have moved forward in time, unaware of each other in the present. I am focused on what lies in front of me, searching for my next story to tell. I know it will come.

EXERCISES

Learn to focus on moments, as opposed to events. New writers begin with dry narration of events, which often include superfluous leading and trailing information. Find the dramatic core of a particular scene: a point of conflict or one character's reaction to another. Write the action for only that moment. See how much of the surrounding detail becomes insignificant.

Invite inspiration through regular practice. Allow yourself a daily ritual of free writing on any subject or idea. While learning to ignore the stifling voice of the self-editor, the mind will relax and explore those dangerous places that you typically avoid. Once you are armed with the craft of storytelling, your writing will assume a more concrete and cogent form.

XI. Life Support

==

"Knowing what you cannot do is more important than knowing what you can do."
– Lucille Ball

My target reader lets me know when I get too tricky. She puts down my prose and tells me to cut it out. She is a reader and a friend, and I cannot win without her approval. She is tireless. She is honest. She reads when she'd rather not, and she has read this book too. I dedicate every book to her, and she is mine. You can't have her. Go find your own.

REALITY CHECK

Most published authors have a job, and it is not writing stories, novels, and memoirs. They supplement their income with other work. Many have day jobs in unrelated fields. Some teach or mentor writers. Others are journalists or professional writers in the industry. These endeavors can support a family, especially professional industry writing.

Corporations pay large fees for the content of booklets, brochures, websites, and presentation materials. If a writer has a gift for succinct and clear prose – a skill everyone should entertain – that talent can reap financial rewards.

At the end of the day, a writer dreams of seeing his work in print. Early in his career, this is often a chance occurrence. Many writers stockpile manuscripts. They salvage old ideas to create new projects or finally publish old stories when the time is ripe. Some writers seek alternative writing projects that promote their unsold stories. They ghost write or submit stories and editorials to free and charitable organizations.

Typically, success is a slow building process. It grows from small publishing victories, until the writer gains a certain mastery of his craft and a reputation in the business. This requires a great deal of patience and determination, but one day, after many years of labor, a writer is lucky to be recognized as an overnight success. Even young literary prodigies were writing for a long time, before we learned their names.

Regardless of a writer's career status, he continues to write. He aspires to elevate his prose throughout his life. He has a passion for the written word, and his love for writing drives him to learn the craft and expand his art. Much of learning to write is trial and error, and he persists through that struggle. As it has been said, half the battle in life is continuing to show up. A writer knows that he will always write, if merely for the love of the process. What else is he going to do with all those crazy ideas?

REJECTION

Rejection is an inevitable part of the business. With few exceptions, writers garner countless rejections on their path to success. It is called 'paying your dues,' but it is not a bill that anyone wants to pay. Dedicated writers work very hard at their art and craft. They'd rather skip paying their dues. It smacks of a fraternity hazing, although it is not done intentionally. No one is sitting at the publishing house, taking note of how many rejection slips a potential author acquires. The writer's words eventually reach an acceptable level, and then it lucks into the right hands. The equation is talent, craft, and timing.

As a writer climbs the ladder of success, he is sometimes shunned by both sides. Publishers will pigeonhole a writer based on his previous work, while unpublished writers tend to marginalize successful writers based on their ability to market their work to the public. The former situation is solved by penning convincing work, and the latter is not a problem. I have been shunned by unpublished writers who "would never do what I do," which amounts to writing a successful novel. So-called artistic integrity is the last refuge of the failed artist.

Take rejection for what it is. A particular work did not fit in that place at that moment in time. This happens for a variety of reasons that may or may not reflect upon the quality of the prose. If the same response keeps popping up, with no supporting success, it is time to elevate the prose. When a writer actively works and strives for more, he or she will achieve their best work.

SEEKING HELP

It is nearly impossible to work in a vacuum. To get to the next level, emerging writers seek advice outside of the publishing industry. Editors and agents don't have time to give the necessary feedback

Most writers begin public exposure inside writer's groups. Feedback is always useful if it is the unfettered response of a reader, but revealing new work to other struggling writers creates shades of gray. I have never had much success in writers' groups. While they can be great social gatherings, I question their candidness and their ability to instruct. They know too much about the story form but not enough to make a difference.

My writing mentor took me over the hump. He is an accomplished writer on his own and knows the path to success. He showed me what I did well and where I needed work. This advice was not based on the market aspects of writing but the elements of a good story. Find a good mentor of your own, someone who understands the story form and the tools of the craft. The rest is up to you.

FINALLY

My personal path to publishing went through many rejections, too many sleepless nights, and a relentless dedication to the craft. I have read, studied, and dissected the story form. I fought with dysgraphia to put cogent words on paper. I have always believed that a great story will rise to the top of a slush pile and make people take notice. I have seen evidence that a solid story is appreciated and read by the public, regardless of the size of the press and its marketing budget. I believe that the reading public is alive and well.

I hold readers and stories in high regard, but mostly, I love the moments alone in my writing space, when ideas take shape and precipitate into words. For me, no finer time exists during the life of a story.

This experience is not unique. As I converse with other authors, I hear similar stories of rejection and struggle along the way, but all writers love to write. A common relentlessness exists among writers to get their thoughts into the most concise and compelling words. In the end, it is always about the words.

Try to put aside the noise of rejection and the buzz of market pressures. Concentrate on what it is that you want to say in words. I often offer this advice to emerging writers. It summarizes what I believe:

Write every day, be brave, and enjoy!

Appendix

*"Few things are harder to put up with than
the annoyance of a good example."*
– Mark Twain

THE FINAL INGREDIENT
by Christopher Klim

Nola J's Friday Specials
Sesame-Encrusted Salmon in a Wasabi-Saki Paste,
with New Zealand Mussels
Roasted Capon in a Tarragon-Chardonnay sauce,
with Spring Vegetables
Veal Nola with Cracked Crab and Tomatoes

When the call came from prison, I was lecturing Faith MacPherson again. The waiters lingered by the salad prep, working the tongs through the spicy greens. The dishwashers paused over sudsy piles of flowered china, the steam moistening their hair. They believed I enjoyed criticizing her. I saw that look in their eyes. They thought I was a bitch, but I loathed having to spell things out for Faith. I hoped she'd aspire to perfection on her own.

"The mousse cake was garnished with fruit." I watched her shrug her shoulders. Pink streaks accented her braided hair. She wore a flaming orange tube top beneath her apron. What could she know about presentation and style? "It is supposed to be painted with cocoa and caramel sauce."

"Everyone does it like that." She smirked as if she'd reinvented the Caesar Salad. "I decided to go with sliced orange and kiwi and give it an island flair."

"This is Princeton, not a luau at Club Med." I recalled her resume—excellent credentials, a woman to take under my wing. This business grinds up women like discount chuck. I hesitated to embrace my failure.

"I thought the citrus complimented the rich flavors."

"I don't need ideas. I need consistency." I drummed the facts into her head. A person saw magic emerge from the kitchen, but in reality, the menu was set far in advance. A kitchen required skilled chefs who recreated the same illusion with pinpoint accuracy. "Customers want the Crème Brulee to appear exactly as the dozen times before. Do you know what I am saying? Exactly the same."

"That's a bore." She blew her pink bangs off her eyes.

I wanted to smack her. That's how my mother would have handled it. This was my kitchen. The title on the engraved menus bore my name. Faith was my assistant, my hire, and my mistake. I'd gone out on a limb, selecting her above more qualified chefs.

"Ms. Jones?" Ralph held the cordless phone from the front desk. He burst into the kitchen, noticing the sluggish activity. He locked onto Faith and me near the large stainless steel doors to the cooler, then rolled his eyes. He knew she was in trouble again.

"You have a call." Ralph stepped softly, the soles of his Italian loafers kissing the tile floor. "It seems urgent. Should I inform him that you are involved?"

I snatched the phone from his hand, commanding Faith to wait with a single glance. It was after ten and only three couples remained in the dining room. If I wanted, I could make the kitchen grind to a halt. "Hello?"

"Is this Nola Jones?" The caller's voice splintered and

twanged at the edges, like a stretched rubber band about to pop.

"Yes."

"Thank God. I am having an awful time with this dessert. It's coming out all wrong."

"Who is this?"

"Ben Kuppek. I cook at the prison."

"Trenton?" I figured he wanted food shipped for a prison function. "I only cater in-house."

"No, no. I need to make Zabaglione."

"It's simple: eggs, sugar, Marsala." I prepared to hang up and resume my argument. Faith bit her nails. I'd told her to stop last week. She caught my glare and stuffed her hands beneath her apron.

"Just whip it together over a low heat," I said.

"I am getting it all wrong."

I paused to concentrate on the caller. He was an institutional cook. I imagined huge pots of chili brewing in a kitchen with utensils resembling pitchforks and shovels. Zabaglione was deceivingly simple, like carbonara and hollandaise, something a rookie took for granted and blew in grand fashion.

"Should I send you directions?" I asked.

Kuppek sighed a chef's sigh, as if he'd burnt the apricot passion soufflé or, in his case, the instant cake mix. An aspiring chef pleaded for assistance. I wished Faith asked for help. Even the waiters saw her struggle.

"Would you like me to demonstrate?"

"Could you?" He responded, a desperate lift in his voice.

"It will be my pleasure."

"Armi said you were the only one."

"Who?"

"Hayden Armistice."

"Hayden Armistice?" The name stopped me cold. I knew Armistice. He loved my Zabaglione. I'd scribbled it on the board one night, because I wanted the challenge. Armistice was big money from Princeton. He used to make special orders. Requests like that turned me on, so I obliged whenever he posted a reservation. It had shocked me to learn that the courts convicted him.

"Turns out he's got good taste," Kuppek said.

"The restaurant's closed on Monday. We do prep for the week. You can come to my kitchen."

"That's cutting it close."

"What do you mean?"

"It's part of his last meal. He's set to die on Monday."

My eyes turned away from Faith. I pictured Armistice in his Burberry suit and gold cufflinks, the essence of refined existence. "I didn't realize."

"I kind of wanted to get it right."

"It's the honorable thing." I often wondered how my meals finished the day. This one would be the finish for Hayden Armistice. "Let me think. Weekends are crazy."

"I understand. I used to manage a little Italian joint on the highway."

I let his comment pass unmolested. "Tomorrow is a regular menu. Sunday is the Thompson Banquet. Everything will be on autopilot. I can show you then."

"Super. It will give me time to practice."

"You must practice."

I hung up on Kuppek and refocused on Faith, but the specter of Hayden Armistice pervaded my thoughts. I fought to recapture the thrust of my argument.

Faith leaned against the counter by the food proces-
sors. She slunk back to the spot in front of me. She reminded
me of a cat I owned once. That animal harbored a lot of bad
ideas too. One involved scratching the hide on my leather
couch. I deposited it at the SPCA so it might reconsider.

"Fruit with the cake," I said aloud. The help had lost
interest. Waiters charged through the door with trays of dirty
dishes, depositing them near the sloppy water. They thought
about counting their tips and hitting the road.

"It doesn't work?" Faith lowered her head, her
confidence waning.

"It cheapens the presentation. It's a shortcut."

"Shortcut?"

"Shortcuts are for diners." I hadn't intended to insult
diners. I respected them. They handled a few dozen ingredients, mixing and matching to fill a menu as dense as a
Michener novel.

"I should have asked you first."

"You may ask, but the answer will probably be no."

She shied away. I thought that I might have been too
harsh, but she stopped and looked back, her pink braids
snapping around her head. "May I have Sunday off?"

I felt the punch sapped out of me. My hair was sweaty
on my scalp, and my makeup felt grungy and exhausted. I
needed a spell in the hot tub and a long shower. "Sunday is
the Thompson Banquet."

"I heard you say it was on autopilot."

I divided my thoughts between who was in and who
was out, and Faith just passed to the out list. She mustered no
drive or courage to ride out the storm. I dismissed her with a
wave. "Work it out with Gerald."

Thompson Banquet
Moroccan Fish Soup Tangine Style
Smoke Salmon on Toast with Capers
Montasio Cheese Frico stuffed with Arugula
Angel Hair with Herb Pesto and Tomatoes
Baby Lamb Chops encrusted in Garlic and Herbs
Griddle-Crisped Chicken with Olives and Polenta
Assorted Pastries

On Sunday evening, I stood in Ben Kuppek's Chambersburg apartment, avoiding the madness of my kitchen. Dennis Thompson was a patron of Nola J's since I opened the doors ten years ago. I was sure his banquet rolled without a hitch. I'd left the details to my other assistant, Gerald Basque. He was a quiet man, older than I, with scant flare but deft precision in the kitchen. A real wizard with the knife, he dressed meats better than any chef I'd encountered. He deserved more of my attention. Soon he might be my only assistant.

I whipped out my cell phone and dialed the restaurant. I'd arrived early on Sunday, set up the appetizers, and finished the soup. I left the meats to the blade master but departed before he showed. It wasn't like Gerald to be late.

"Good evening, Nola J's." Ralph answered the phone with contrived dazzle. He saw my cell number on the caller ID.

"This is the chef," I said, our little joke. "Is my assistant in?"

"Yup, the pots are running over."

"How's Thompson?"

"Like a pig in mud," he whispered, "cheeks full of Frico as we speak. Shall I go ask?"

I glanced at my watch, matching it against the tacky clock in Kuppek's undersized and poorly stocked kitchen. "Three courses down already?"

"They are licking the tablecloths tonight."

"Should I get back?"

"We can survive a night without you. You might consider asking Mr. Short Order out for a drink."

I scanned Kuppek as he entered his narrow kitchen. He stood beside painted tiles of herbs and spices. The tarragon looked like sage, which resembled rosemary. At least, they were green and buoyant, unlike Kuppek who appeared gray and weary from smoking. After viewing his pathetic kitchen, the first thing I asked him to do was to put out the cigarette, now.

"No such luck," I said.

"No sparks?" Ralph quipped.

"I don't think our ingredients would blend well."

"Too spicy?"

"Too stale." I watched Kuppek smile. His hair shined, thick and wet, permanently locked in the 70's. "Call me if there's trouble at the shop."

"Right-o captain."

I jumped into the recipe. I whisked the eggs and sugar in a double boiler, gently adding the Marsala to the fold. "Bring the temperature slowly to 160 degrees. Too fast, and you won't achieve maximum volume. Too hot and you'll curdle it. Understand?"

Kuppek nodded, impressed by my talent at the stove. He seemed to grasp the process, but he held the whisk like a crowbar. Worse yet, he mixed unevenly, stopping at times. He demonstrated no inclination for the subtleties of cooking.

"Keep it going." I said encouragingly. "Are you friends with Armistice?"

"Friendly. Sometimes, we sit after dinner. No one visits him."

"What do you talk about?"

"Good food and wine. He knows a lot."

He frowned into the pot, watching the bubbles recede into the liquid. "I should have seen this coming. Usually it's shrimp cocktail and filet mignon. Killers don't often come from million dollar estates."

I assumed control of the whisk, vigorously attacking the mixture as we spoke. I possessed the ability to divide my mind between tasks. To survive in the kitchen, you must handle a minimum of three simultaneous operations. "I can't believe they're executing him."

"I can."

I thought he sounded pitiless. Armistice was, after all, another human being. I reduced the flame before the liquid spoiled. "He spared his dying wife more pain. Don't you think that shows compassion?"

Kuppek's head kicked back like the lid to a trashcan. "He's done it before."

"What do you mean?"

"He married two other older women before this one. Both were sickly like the third." Kuppek leered. "Both died unnaturally."

"You're joking."

"Armi helped things along."

"How?"

"Poison. Slipped it into their medication."

The conversation fizzled. It took an hour and a half to

coax Kuppek into producing recognizable foam. He thanked me profusely, and I evacuated his ashtray apartment, relieved to find my silver Jaguar untouched in the street.

I pressed the speed dial for the restaurant. "Where are we?"

"Assorted Pastries, Ma'am." Ralph spoke as if reciting the menu for the Queen of England. He got on my nerves.

"Success?"

"Four star, I'd say."

"Not five?"

"One complaint about fatty lamb chops."

I was mortified. "Fatty?"

"Yes."

"How did Gerald let that happen?"

"Gerald? Sunday is Faith's night."

"I thought they switched?"

"Who told you that? She came in late as always."

I hung up without saying good-bye. I was going to kill her, throttle her neck until her pink hair turned a fuchsia shade of blue. It was all over but the paperwork for unemployment.

Monday
Restaurant Closed
Call for Reservations

I thrashed around my kitchen. I cooked when I was angry. I liked the pungent spices and the feel of the blade in my hands as I pulverized the meats and vegetables in my path. It restored sanity to a world without order.

Veal shanks simmered in a pot of vegetables for Osso
Buco. Duck poached for Wednesday's confit. A pot of trout
and herb soup and another with mushrooms and lentils
melded on the stove. Soup tasted best after a day or two. I
envisioned the weekly specials coming together. I gathered
my strength, feeling the toxins in my veins subside. I can run
this place by myself. I don't need help.

Faith entered as the phone rang. I was tempted not to
pick it up and fire her on the spot. With one hand on the
phone, I scanned her tie-dye outfit and beaded purse. I felt
cold. Clean out your closet and remove your wardrobe of
knives before sundown.

"It's a disaster," Ben Kuppek said over the line. He
sounded desperate again.

"Calm down. What's going on?"

"I can't get it. A dead man's waiting for dessert, and I
can't pull it off."

"What's it look like?"

"Soup."

"It collapsed. Toss it and start over."

"I have done it three times already." Kuppek coughed,
then wheezed. The receiver fuzzed in my ear.

"The heat's too high."

"I know that, but any lower and the flame goes out."

I pictured the bulky institutional burner—great for
boiling a pot of macaroni and cheese for one hundred men.
Hayden Armistice would never taste my Zabaglione again. "I
have a portable propane burner. You can bend candles over it
without melting the wax."

"Thank God, you're an angel."

"I'll be there in thirty minutes."

I disconnected and stared at Faith. She stood at attention. Word had drifted back about the fatty lamb and my reaction. Her hands fidgeted with her purse strap. She assumed the worst, and she was right.

"I have an emergency," I barked. "Watch everything."

I expected the dishes to be ruined by the time I returned.

Hayden Armistice's Last Meal
Oysters on the Half Shell
Pear Salad with Mixed Greens,
Walnuts, and Gorgonzola
Skate with Black Butter
Salmi of Squab
Zabaglione

I parked my Jaguar beside the mosaic on the prison's outer wall. A mural of joyous faces roamed beneath barbed-wire and watchtowers encased in bulletproof glass. A guard tilted his head in my direction. I smiled and yanked my instruments from the seat.

Ben Kuppek intercepted me at the gate. A guard patted me down and escorted us to the galley. I tried not to focus on the electric gates and weapons around me, retaining my composure. The place smelled like loneliness, like a kitchen after midnight when everyone's left and you sit beside the cold burners with a glass of sherry. If you shift too suddenly, you create an echo, the imprint of your existence bouncing back at you.

I brushed Ben aside, set up the burner, and rose the

savory foam in ten minutes. Everything I employed—the whisk, double boiler, the very ingredients—came from my kitchen. I refused to leave another detail to chance.

Hayden Armistice sat at one end of a long table. I emerged from the galley holding the Zabaglione. Kuppek had tried to take the fluted glass from my hands, but I stopped him. It became a matter of pride. This was my creation.

I set the dessert in front of Armistice and placed a silver spoon beside it on a linen napkin. Armistice looked up. His eyes were the thing I remembered, deep brown like warm dark mocha. His eyebrows and mustache looked exquisitely groomed, black and peppered with gray. His clothes were prison issue denim, complete with stenciled name and number on the chest. I understood the indignity of being poorly dressed when you knew better. I felt sorry for him. He'd die in those clothes. I was glad I'd packed the silver spoon and crystal.

"Miss Jones," he said, "or is it Ms. Jones."

"Miss is fine."

"I was hoping you'd come. Please, sit."

I saw Kuppek chat with the guard by the swinging doors to the galley. They seemed as unthreatened by Armistice as I was by Faith MacPherson. I slid a plastic chair from the table.

Armistice dipped the spoon into the glass, retrieving a moderate portion of foam. He slid it in his mouth and shut his eyes. I saw them flutter ever so slightly behind the lids. The simplest ingredients conjured ecstasy on the palate.

"Marvelous," he said.

"Thank you." This was the moment a chef rarely gets, the pure enjoyment of one's craft.

"I wish you had prepared the entire meal."

"No one asked."

The corners of his mouth turned down for a moment, then lifted as he savored another spoonful. "The Zabaglione is treat enough."

"Thanks again."

"You have the knack. I regret not visiting your restaurant lately."

"I noticed you stopped coming around, before I heard about the trial."

"It was a taxing affair. My stomach couldn't handle more than crackers and chicken broth."

"I understand."

"But that's behind me now." He placed the spoon on the table and stared across the dinning hall. I wanted to turn around, but I knew there were only drab tables and monotonous walls at my back. His mind wandered. He still looked hungry. I suspected that if I dove into my repertoire of finest meals, he'd remain unsatisfied.

When he returned, his face appeared heavy. He carried baggage from wherever he'd been. "Are you going to ask the question?"

"What question?" I had an inkling to what he referred.

"Everyone wants to know, but you are too refined to ask. I can tell by your cooking."

"I don't want to trouble you."

"But you are curious."

He was right. I wanted to know why a man with everything went too far. I looked at the dead man, as Kuppek called him. He appeared aloof and unthreatening. What lurked inside? His previous wives had been exhumed and examined for traces of arsenic and morphine. I already knew the contents of Hayden's system at death: eggs, sugar, Marsala, and the lethal injections used to first sedate him, then bring him down.

"My wives were near the end," he said. "I tried to alleviate their pain."

I held still. It was painfully obvious I'd hear his confession.

"But you cannot push things toward fruition," he said. "If I am guilty of anything, it is forcing the inevitable."

The duck confit still simmered when I returned, but the soups and Osso Buco were set aside in good order. I lifted the plastic and poked the veal shanks with a fork. Tender and ripe with flavor. The clock edged toward midnight. Hayden Armistice's stay on earth approached expiration.

Faith gathered the ingredients for Double Chocolate Sponge Cake. Most desserts I bought from a trusted Pennsylvania bakery, but a few I still prepared on the premises to keep the menu honest. As she leaned over the counter, I noticed her pink hair restored to an even brown.

She held an egg in the air, poised to crack it open, but as I covered the veal, she stopped mid stride. "Is it right?"

I tossed the fork in the dish bin, hearing it clank against the rigid steel. "The Osso Buco will be a hit on Wednesday."

"Am I working that night?" She faced me. Her cheeks were scrunched and red. She verged on tears.

I hoped she didn't crush the egg in her hand. "I admit I was going to fire you."

"I know. Everyone told me."

"You have disappointed me."

"I hear it in your voice."

Her admission stunned me. I didn't hear myself speak. I was driven and successful. I mowed down roadblocks, even when the roadblocks were other people. "I expected too much."

"I am sorry I disappointed you." She began to cry. "Before I came here, I'd read about you in the New York Times. I wanted to impress you."

"You stand somewhere between a cook and a chef. You must decide which you want to be."

"A chef like you. Should I pack up and leave?"

I saw how easily she was going to relent. I'd fired better chefs for giving out free meals or moonlighting at other restaurants. One waived a butcher's knife at me but refused to follow me into the dining room and break protocol. I know a great chef when I see one. I believed Faith contained those ingredients, and I refused to let her fail.

"Stop what you're doing. I'll show you how to make Chocolate Zabaglione."

Her face went blank, an empty chalkboard to be filled in the fashion I chose. Her tears ceased. She rested the egg on the counter. Amazingly, it neither rolled off or away. "But that recipe won't stand overnight?"

"When I am through, you'll be able to repeat it for the Wednesday special."

She wiped her eyes with the back of her wrist.

"Master that," I said, "and I'll teach you a few others."

The End.

CHARACTER SKETCH

Sketches for *The Final Ingredient*
by Christopher Klim

Name:

Nola Jones.

Body Specifics:

In my mind, Nola is a 42 year old mulatto woman with pinkish tan skin toward the fair. She has light brown long wavy hair. I didn't want to make race an issue. So I let those interesting details go. She is the shortest person in the kitchen. She is average in build, but trim from constantly moving. Her upper arms are strong, and she has useful hips. A large and heavy bowl of ingredients fits snugly against her side to stir with a thick wooden ladle. She has varicose veins on her calves from constantly pounding tile kitchen floors. She never finds comfortable enough shoes.

Body Language:

Nola doesn't hunch, slouch, cower, whimper, or sigh. She is direct. She stands straight. If you came at her quickly, she'd hold her position to the last second and surprise you with a stunning deflection. She is compact and makes efficient moves. Larger people work harder than her to accomplish the same tasks.

Presentation:

·   I will forever picture Nola in her working whites, conjuring her meals like a high priestess of food, yet a witch doctor of spice and ingredients. Her hair is pulled tightly in a ponytail, as steam rises from an exotic reduction and the burner fires with the aura of incredible scents. Her clothes are well kept and no doubt of fine quality, but I never get to see them. I am merely a worker in her kitchen, observing her. She is in the kitchen before and after anyone else. No one catches her dressing into her coverall. In the scenes outside the kitchen, she dons a large white apron. Maybe Stan Kuppek saw her clothes. Ask him.

Background:

Nola was classically trained, paid her dues, and fought her way through a male dominated business. She no doubt endured and avoided a certain amount of prejudice and occasionally took advantage of her uniqueness. She is determined to avoid mistakes. She partly savored the errors of her peers, knowing it separated her from the pack. She worked hard to earn and finance her own restaurant in a prestigious community.

Psyche:

She understands and respects the hierarchy of the kitchen and expects everyone else to respect it as well. As a meal comes to fruition, any personal transgression is forgiven, as long as the meal is plated to perfection. Like a surgeon above an open patient, the moment is now. No excuses are accepted. She has been hardened by a tough industry.

Strengths & Weaknesses:

Positive: highly competent, undaunted, savvy, and relentless.

Negative: prideful, rigid, and unforgiving of human frailty.

Motivation:

Nola wants perfection and her ambition drives her to the brink of failure with a young understudy, yet by nature, she is constantly searching for an answer. At a critical moment, her pride brings her face to face with a condemned man. She sees a bit of herself in the killer and is changed by the encounter.

During the story, her intolerance sabotages her passion to succeed, until she achieves a deeper understanding. She summons compassion to solve the crisis with the intern, rather than dismissing her. The addition of compassion becomes the final and winning ingredient.

SCENE & SEQUEL ANALYSIS

Plot analysis for *The Final Ingredient* by Christopher Klim

Nola Jones is a successful owner and chef of a Princeton restaurant. She hired Faith as one of her assistants, hoping to instill her knowledge of and dedication to the craft. Nola is relentless yet usually right. When things go awry with Faith, Nola faces the unsavory possibility of her own failure.

Life gets complicated for Nola, when she is asked to demonstrate the dessert for a condemned man's last meal. The condemned man and the failing assistant draw parallels. When Nola is drawn into the man's confession, she learns a bit about herself in the process.

The story is presented in four scenes and a single intermediate sequel.

Scene: Nola confronts assistant chef in restaurant.

Objective: Nola wants to fashion the assistant in her mold.
Problem: Faith is failing and making Nola look bad.
Conflict: Faith is headstrong, and the women argue.
Outcome: Faith asks for a day off, demonstrating her lack of intuition and drive.

Scene: Nola teaching prison chef to make dessert.

Objective: Nola must demonstrate technique for
             condemned man's last meal.
Problem: Tight schedule; prisoner to die on Monday.
Conflict: Nola must leave restaurant on Saturday night
             during banquet.
Outcome: Faith makes mistakes during banquet.

Sequel: Nola in kitchen, determining Faith's fate.

Cognition: Should Nola fire Faith?
Emotion: Nola's angry and senses her own failure.
Decision: Nola determines to fire Faith.

Scene: Nola prepares dessert for condemned man.

Objective: Nola plans to fire Faith.
Problem: Nola must leave for prison to create dessert.
Conflict: Nola's pride leads her to hear a condemned
             man's confession.
Outcome: Nola sees herself in the condemned man.

Scene: Nola confronts assistant a final time.

Objective: Deal with assistant.
Problem: Faith flawlessly manages her final assignment;
             exhibits contrition.
Conflict: Nola questions her part in Faith's failure and
             becomes uncertain of her decision to fire Faith.
Outcome: Nola identifies her unforgiving drive as part of
             the problem and determines to add compassion
             and understanding to help Faith grow.

SHORT STORY QUERY LETTER

Query letter for short story *The Final Ingredient*

Jane Doe, Editor
Famous Short Story Weekly
Submissions & Mostly Rejections
100 Lexington Avenue
New York, NY 100010

Dear Ms. Doe:

    I am a photojournalist and an award-winning fiction writer. My first novel, JESUS LIVES IN TRENTON, was published in 2002.
    In my latest short story, THE FINAL INGREDIENT, a master chef determines the fate of an incompetent employee, while preparing a condemned man's last meal.
    As a former assistant to a master chef, I demonstrate the inner workings of a topnotch professional kitchen. I hope you enjoy my work, and I look forward to your response.

Sincerely,
Christopher Klim

PS: Please dispose of my materials after review.

NOVEL QUERY LETTER

Query Letter for the novel *Jesus Lives in Trenton*

Dear Mr. Jones, Senior Editor:

I am an award-winning fiction writer and a photojournalist. JESUS LIVES IN TRENTON is the story of Boot Means, a photojournalist who gets in over his head while using a mystical event to make a name for himself, but by chance, Boot reconnects with the father he never knew. Set in the desperate urban landscape of Trenton, NJ, this mainstream social satire delves into the heady world of TV evangelism and the seamy underworld of cult organizations.

I am a long time Trenton resident. I believe that the satirical juxtaposition of urban decay, displaced children, the thirst for grace, and TV ministries is ripe for our time. The novel is completed and about 80,000 words long. I have sent sample chapters in the hope of increasing your interest in my work.

Sincerely,
Christopher Klim

PS: Please dispose of materials after review.

NOVEL SYNOPSIS

Novel Synopsis for *Jesus Lives in Trenton*

Jesus Lives in Trenton
a novel
by
Christopher Klim

Boot Means is a photojournalist who gets in over his head while using a mystical event to make a name for himself, but by chance, he reconnects with the father he never knew. Set in the desperate urban landscape of Trenton, NJ, this mainstream social satire takes Boot into the heady world of TV evangelism and the seamy underworld of cult organizations.

Why would Jesus appear in Trenton, a forgotten wreck of a city? Boot Means doesn't care, but he will use the event for everything it's worth. Boot is twenty-four years old and a self-made photographer. Raised as a foundling, he has little to call his own. He plans to create a name for himself as a photo-journalist, yet suffering as the low man for a failing local tabloid, he stands on the verge of being laid-off. Just as Boot seems out of time and money, Jesus' image is sighted on a local billboard. Boot follows one miraculous claim after another, muscling his way into the daily gossip page and ultimately more exposure than he can handle.

As Boot works the Jesus story into the national spotlight, people arrive from out of town, not the least of which are the leaders of two evangelistic ministries with competing agendas. Melanie Dove, a former pop/gospel singer turned preacher, wants to use the Jesus of Trenton to inflate her sagging television ministry. Paul Andujar, a reformed murderer, wants to expand his prison ministry at Trenton State Prison. Boot covers the bitter rivals and, lured by the possibility of greater success, gets duped into helping Dove tarnish Andjuar's reputation. By the time Boot realizes his error, he must lie to preserve his job at the paper.

Boot is unaware that his father, Charles Goodner, is alive and well. Charles has spotted Boot on Dove's national Sunday TV broadcast, and just as Boot's career reaches the breaking point, Charles arrives at Boot's doorstep. Boot is headstrong and fiercely independent. Boot rejects Charles and family, and in the end, Boot sees his lies exposed and his career derailed. He must learn to forgive the past, and in the final scene, he leaves town with his wounded integrity to join his new family in Texas.

SHORT STORY TITLE PAGE & MANUSCRIPT

The first page of prose for a short story or article is the title page. Contact information is placed in the upper left corner, and the upper right corner holds the word count and the rights for sale. The actual title appears one third of the way down the page, followed by a standard break of three lines before the body of the text.

The following example is the beginning of the short story, *The Final Ingredient*, in acceptable format. The remaining pages are formatted like the second page. No page number appears on the first page, although it is assumed to be page number one.

Christopher Klim
PO Box 11
Titusville, NJ 08560
www.ChristopherKlim.com
ChristopherKlim@erols.com
<phone number>

3500 words
first rights

The Final Ingredient

Nola J's Friday Specials:
Sesame-Encrusted Salmon in a
Wasabi-Saki Paste,
with New Zealand Mussels
Roasted Capon in a Tarragon-Chardonnay
sauce, with Spring Vegetables
Veal Nola with Cracked Crab and Tomatoes

When the call came from prison, I
was lecturing Faith MacPherson again. The
waiters lingered by the salad prep,
working the tongs through the spicy
greens. The dishwashers paused over sudsy
piles of flowered china, the steam

moistening their hair. They believed I
enjoyed criticizing her. I saw that look
in their eyes. They thought I was a
bitch, but I loathed having to spell
things out for Faith. I hoped she'd
aspire to perfection on her own.

"The mousse cake was garnished with
fruit." I watched her shrug her
shoulders. Pink streaks accented her
braided hair. She wore a flaming orange
tube top beneath her apron. What could
she know about presentation and style?
"It's supposed to be painted with cocoa
and caramel sauce."

"Everyone does it like that." She
smirked as if she'd reinvented the Caesar
Salad. "I decided to go with sliced
orange and give it an island flair."

NOVEL TITLE PAGE & MANUSCRIPT

A book length manuscript requires its own title page. The title, contact information, and word count are placed one third of the way down the page and in the center. The actual prose begins on the next page.

The following example shows a novel title page and the first page of the manuscript for the sequel to *Jesus Lives in Trenton*, entitled *Everything Burns*. The title page is not included in the running page count.

Everything Burns

by

Christopher Klim
PO Box 11
Titusville, NJ 08530
www.ChristopherKlim.com
ChristopherKlim@erols.com
<phone number>

60,000 words

CHAPTER 1
Knocking Them Down

Boot Means skidded his motorcycle to the curb and hopped off. Ladder trucks hummed outside a line of shops in Concho's commercial district. A hardware store on Harp Street stood gutted, and wisps of gray smoke crept from the second floor apartment windows. He was late. The flames were already knocked down. That's how the firemen put it—'knocked down'—as if they'd toppled a big bully and left him for dead.

Bibliography, Film & Music

Bickham, Jack. *Scene & Sequel: The Two Keys to Strong Plots*, Writer's Digest, 1990.

Block, Lawrence. *Writing the Novel: from Plot to Print*, Writer's Digest Books, 1979.

Chapnick, Howard. *Truth Needs No Alley*, University of Missouri Press, 1994.

Clancy, Tom. *Hunt for Red October*, Berkley 1997.

Dickens, Charles. *A Christmas Carol*, Bantam Classics, 1999.

Ellison, Ralph. *Invisible Man*, Vintage Books, 1995

Fitzgerald, F. Scott. *The Great Gatsby*, Scribner Classics, 1996.

Fleischer, Richard, and Masuda, Toshio. *Tora! Tora! Tora!*, Twentieth Century Fox,1970.

Gilliam, Terry. *Twelve Monkeys*, Universal Studios, 1996.

Harris, Thomas. *Silence of the Lambs*, St. Martin's Press, 1988.

Harrison, Kathryn. *Exposure*, Random House, 1993.

Herbert, Frank. *Dune*, Berkley, 1965.

Holt, Lawrence Robert. *How to Publish, Promote, and Sell Your Own Book*, St. Martin's Press, 1985.

Irving, John. *The World According to Garp*, Random House, 1976.

Jenkins, Jerold, and Stanton, Anne. *Publish to Win*, Rhodes & Easton, 1997.

Junger, Sebastian. *The Perfect Storm*, Harper, 1998.

Kennedy, Thomas. *Realism & Other Illusions*, Wordcraft of Oregon, 2002.

King, Stephen. *On Writing*, Pocket Books, 2000.

Klim, Christopher. *Jesus Lives in Trenton*, Creative Arts Books, 2002.

Marius, Richard. *After the War*, Knopf, 1992.

McCarthy, Cormac. *All the Pretty Horses*, Knopf, 1992.

Palahniuk, Chuck. *Fight Club*, Norton & Co., 1996.

Pop, Iggy. *Avenue B*, Virgin Records, 1999.

Spencer, Bret. *Are We Not Men?*, Arcade, 1996.

Strunk, William, and White, E.B. *The Elements of Style*, McMillan, 1979.

Swain, Dwight. *Creating Characters: How to Build Story People*, Writer's Digest Books, 1990.

About the Author

Christopher Klim worked on observation and exploration satellites for the space program, until departing for the private sector to develop leading-edge communications technologies. He now teaches and mentors emerging writers. He is the senior editor of *Writers Notes Magazine* and primary architect of www.WritersNotes.com. In his lectures, writings, and workshops, this award-winning storyteller entertains with contemporary tales that extend the American experience while transcending the ordinary. His first novel *Jesus Lives in Trenton* was released to critical acclaim.

Contact the author:
c/o Hopewell Publications
PO Box 11
Titusville, NJ 08560-0011
ChristopherKlim@erols.com

www.ChristopherKlim.com
www.WritersNotes.com

Index

agent, 99
   literary, 99
   referral, 101
   reverse search, 101
artist vs. artisan, 3
author
   about the, 157
   biography, 99
basic order, 80
Bickham, Jack, 60
Block, Lawrence, 60
character
   antagonist, 26
   applying to story, 24
   background, 21
   body language, 21
   body specifics, 20
   confidante, 26
   foil, 26
   main, 10
   motivation, 23
   names, 20
   presentation, 21
   profiling, 25
   protagonist, 26

psyche, 22
sketch, example of, 139
strengths and
   weaknesses, 22
Christie, Agatha, 66
Clancy, Tom, 110
conflict, 58
creativity, 109
Dickens, Charles, 16
drama, 57
Ellison, Ralph, 110
feedback, 82, 118
fine writing, 79
freelancing, 104
Gover, Robert, 64
grammar, 81
Harris, Thomas, 110
Harrison, Kathryn, 16
Herbert, Frank, 45
inspiration, 112
Internet research, 51
Irving, John, 57
Jesus Lives in Trenton, 90,
   145, 152
Kennedy, Thomas E., 5

manuscript, 97
    double-spaced, 97
    format, 97
    left-justified, 98
    margins, 98
    novel example, 151
    page information, 98
    short story example, 148
McCarthy, Cormac, 97
meditation, 109
multiple submissions, 102
novel, what is, 14
plot, 55
    conflict, 58
    construction, 59
    drama, 57
    problems, 58
    scenes and sequels, 59
point of view, 11, 31
    first person, 32
    omniscient, 36
    second person, 33
    selecting character, 39
    standard third person, 37
    third person, 35
    third person singular, 37
Pop, Iggy, 29
query
    letter, 94
    novel example, 145
    process, 102
    response, 103
    short story example, 144
reading aloud, 79
rejection, 117

revisions
    character details, 73
    finishing, 83
    first pass, 70
    openings, 71
    plot details, 72
    presentation, 80
    sentence structure, 76
    setting details, 75
    structure and content, 72
    style, 76
    tone, 76
rewriting, 69
ritual, 7
scene, 60
    analysis example, 142
    conflict, 61
    objective, 61
    order, 65
    outcome, 61
    problem, 61
sequel, 62
    analysis example, 142
    cognition, 62
    decision, 63
    emotion, 63
setting, 12, 43
    applying to story, 47
    future, 45
    lifestyle, 46
    location, 46
    past, 44
    present, 45
    research, 50
    scene manipulation, 49

sex scenes, writing, 111
Shelley, Mary, 66
spelling, 81
story
    endings, 64, 98
    framework, 7
    ideas, 106
    opening, 9
    research, 50
    sequencing, 64
    story question, 11
    structure, 64, 65
    timeline, 13
    transitions, 65
    unwritten code, 52
storyteller, 2

storytelling, 1
synopsis, 96
    example, 146
    The Final Ingredient, 123
title
    story, 90
    title page, 98
tone, 13
voice, finding your, 110
word choice, 77
write what you know, 110
writer's block, 108
www.WritersNotes.com,
    51, 104